CRUCIBLE
MOMENTS

CRUCIBLE MOMENTS

INSPIRING LIBRARY LEADERSHIP

STEVEN J. BELL

EDITOR

MISSION BELL MEDIA

FIRST EDITION

Library of Congress Preassigned Control Number
2015917380

ISBN 978-0-9907300-5-7

MISSION BELL MEDIA

Rolf A. Janke, CEO
Leah Watson, Director of Marketing
Sara Tauber, Editorial Manager
Danielle Hartbrodt, Social Media Marketing Administrator
Mary Jo Scibetta, Production Manager

Produced by Firefly Media Arts, LLC

Contents

About the Editor

Steven J. Bell is the Associate University Librarian for Research and Instructional Services at Temple University. Prior to that he was Director of the Paul J. Gutman Library at Philadelphia University from 1997 to 2006 and the Assistant Director at the Wharton School at the University of Pennsylvania from 1993 to 1996. While at the University of Pennsylvania, Steven earned his Ed.D. with a concentration in Higher Education Leadership. This is the source of his dual passion for leadership and higher education.

As the author of two weekly columns for Library Journal Academic Newswire, "From the Bell Tower" and "Leading From the Library," he has written hundreds of columns about these two subjects, dating back to 2009. He also writes and speaks about academic librarianship, technology change, educational technology, design thinking, and user experience. Steven has keynoted over 40 professional physical and virtual conferences. In addition to numerous published articles, he is a coauthor of the book *Academic Librarianship by Design*. Other accomplishments include cofounding the Blended Librarians Online Learning Community, being a founding blogger of ACRLog, and being a member of the inaugural class of *Library Journal's* Movers & Shakers (2002). Steven also maintains a blog about design and user experience, "Designing Better Libraries." For additional information about Steven J. Bell or links to his projects, see http://stevenbell.info.

What's most exciting for Steven about leadership, at any level, is having the opportunity to take a vision, or even a project, and to try to take it from idea to implementation. He finds excitement in encouraging his colleagues to rally around that idea and bring it to fruition. Although taking the risk to come forward with ideas and influencing others can be a bit terrifying, Steven has learned that it's worth taking the chance. He takes encouragement from many different leaders, rather than having a single favorite, and is always looking for great leadership stories that offer inspiration or lessons from which to learn.

One of the things Steven enjoys about having a library career is the many opportunities to share ideas through articles and speaking engagements. Steven states, "We have a great professional community and I've been fortunate to get to meet many librarians and visit their libraries." What he often hears from his family is to "slow down." To do so, he finds relaxation in activity, whether it's going to the gym or taking a walk or a bike ride. When he is truly motivated to slow down, he will usually garden or just read magazines, which is a favorite pastime and an occupational hazard.

List of Contributors

José A. Aguiñaga	*Glendale Community College*
Steven J. Bell	*Temple University*
Char Booth	*California State University, San Marcos*
Peter Bromberg	*Salt Lake County Library Services*
Jon E. Cawthorne	*West Virginia University*
Trevor A. Dawes	*Washington University in St. Louis*
Patrick José Dawson	*Northern Illinois University*
Irene M. H. Herold	*University of Hawaii at Mānoa*
Eboni A. Johnson	*Oberlin College*
Joshua Kim	*Dartmouth College*
Brian Mathews	*Virginia Tech Libraries*
Kenley Neufeld	*Santa Barbara City College*
Erin T. Smith	*Westminster College*
Maureen Sullivan	*Organization Development Consultant, Maureen Sullivan Associates, Annapolis, MD*
Rosalind Tedford	*Wake Forest University*

About the Contributors

José Aguiñaga, Ed.D., Library Faculty and Faculty Senate President at Glendale Community College, Arizona, began his educational journey with his undergraduate degree from the University of San Diego. After graduation, José completed his MLS at the University of Arizona. After 10 years as an academic librarian he decided to complete his MPA at California State University, Long Beach. Eight years later he earned his Ed.D. from Northern Arizona University. José states, "We live in an age of constant change, this is what excites and invigorates my pursuit for library leadership opportunities." Besides being a librarian, José is an avid San Diego Chargers and Padres fan. When asked to name his favorite leader, José replies decidedly, "That would be my mom."

Char Booth is Associate Dean of the Library at California State University, San Marcos and a faculty member of the ACRL Information Literacy Immersion Institute. Early riser, devoted oceanite, and advocate of radical neutrality, Char Booth explores the integration of pedagogy, research, technology, and design in libraries. Char presents and writes on topics related to the integration of pedagogy, assessment, technology, and design in libraries—she blogs at info-mational, tweets @ charbooth, and her publications include the Ilene F. Rockman Instruction Publication of the Year–winning *Reflective Teaching, Effective Learning: Instructional Literacy for Library Educators* (ALA Editions, 2011) and *Informing Innovation: Tracking Student Interest in Emerging Library Technologies* (ACRL, 2009).

Peter Bromberg is currently learning in his role as Associate Director for Public Services at the Salt Lake County Library, and in his role as a board member for EveryLibrary. When asked to provide a bio, he often jokes that, "I'm just a simple librarian trying to make it in this crazy world." Beneath the joke, though, Peter maintains a deeply held belief—"That we're all doing our best each day to navigate our way through a complex world. The choices we make and the actions we take moment after moment either enrich our own lives and those around us or they don't." Peter feels that leadership is about being increasingly mindful and intentional in our exertion of positive influence and continually learning from our experiences as well as from the perspective and wisdom of others.

Jon E. Cawthorne, Dean of Libraries, West Virginia University, entered the profession in 1993, and since that time, library leadership positions have remained a North Star for his career. He is excited about the opportunities to create an academic library that inspires everyone to participate in a brighter future. Jon states, "Each library position I have held, both in the academic and public spheres, prepared me for my current role, and I couldn't be more grateful." Learning from numerous job changes and uncertain times along his professional path, Jon encourages everyone to persevere through challenges, self-doubt, and any limiting thinking they may encounter. Two leaders that Jon admires are Mahatma Gandhi and Maya Angelou. Gandhi said, "Leaders don't create followers. They create more leaders." And Angelou said, "People will forget what you said, people will forget what you did, but people will never forget how you made them feel." Jon finds his personal inspiration in his friendships, reading, cycling, making pottery, and traveling to new cities and foreign lands. He and his wife enjoy living in Morgantown, West Virginia, with two dogs, and watching their three children grow and make their way in the world.

Trevor A. Dawes is an Associate University Librarian at Washington University in St. Louis. In this role he leads many of the libraries' public services operations. He was previously the Circulation Services Director at the Princeton University Library, and prior to that held several positions at the Columbia University Libraries in New York City. Trevor states, "The nature of the work that our faculty and students are doing is changing (ever more interdisciplinary, data and technology driven) and we need to continue enhancing our skills in order to meet ever-changing needs." He feels that one of the most exciting parts of being a leader is being able to continue developing yourself and also encouraging others to have a positive impact on those with whom they work. Trevor feels that being a leader can be challenging, as leaders need to constantly reinvent themselves.

When thinking about a favorite leader, Trevor looks for the qualities in people that he personally admires. His favorite leader, therefore, is an amalgamation of several people, each of whom has traits that he tries to emulate, and therein he finds great motivation.

Patrick José Dawson, Dean, University Libraries, Northern Illinois University, grew up in New Mexico in a bilingual, bicultural family. Somewhere along the path to earn a Ph.D. in Latin American Studies, librarianship was discovered as a career option. He has no regrets about this change in focus. Patrick feels the exciting thing about leadership is to take an idea, regardless of origin, and help to move this idea into a new program or service that is beneficial to the library user and information seeker. Patrick finds it exciting to see people in the library develop and grow as new leaders. He states, "The terrifying aspect of leadership is fear of failing to make your library relevant and people in the library success-ful." The people who have most influenced Patrick as leaders from their style of leadership to their commitment to social justice are Mahatma Gandhi, Mother Teresa, and Dr. Martin Luther King, Jr. When Patrick needs a way to release cre-ative energy and find relaxation, he finds this opportunity in his motorcycle, hav-ing been a rider since the ripe old age of 13.

Irene M.H. Herold is the University Librarian for Library Services, University of Hawaii at Mānoa. Her Ph.D. is in Managerial Leadership in the Information Professions from Simmons College. In addition to attending three leadership development programs, she was the program director of the College Library Directors' Mentor Program from 2012 to 2013. She was elected the Association of College and Research Libraries vice president/president elect in 2015. Her other publications include a 2015 book on leadership development programs, *Creating Leaders: An Examination of Academic and Research Library Leadership Institutes*, and a coauthored 2014 chapter in *Advances in Librarianship*, called "Mindful Leadership Defined and Explained."

Eboni A. Johnson is a Reference & Instruction Librarian at Oberlin College, where she also earned her B.A. in Africana Studies and English in 1997, "way back when the Internet as we know it today was barely a thing," she jokes. She went on to earn her MLIS from Kent State University in 2003. Eboni feels that leadership can be as terrifying as it is deeply rewarding. She states, "Leadership requires using all kinds of skill sets and both sides of your brain at the same time." She likes to approach leadership from a place of compassion and authenticity, like Dr. Martin Luther King, Jr. When she's not leading or librarian-ing, you can find her playing with wool—turning fluff into yarn, and then knitting the yarn into sweaters or socks. And when she's not doing that, you'll find her training for triathlon. Sometimes she sleeps.

Joshua Kim, Ph.D., is the Director of Digital Learning Initiatives at the Dartmouth Center for the Advancement of Learning. He considers himself an academic library groupie and states, "If the world ran the way it should then the librarians would be running the place." Joshua would rather read books than do anything else and is fortunate to have academic library friends who provide a constant stream of book recommendations and book conversations. He says, "If 'friend of the academic library' were an official job title, then that would be the job I'd want." Joshua is proud to work in a field that has shifted and changed with the fluctuating technological, economic, labor market, and demographic landscape. He is inspired by all the people at colleges and universities whose efforts actually make the place run, but who seldom receive enough credit or appreciation for their work.

Brian Mathews is Associate Dean at the Virginia Tech Libraries. He has also served in leadership positions at the University of California, Santa Barbara and Georgia Tech. Brian was initially drawn to librarianship during the emergence of the Web and the inherent challenges with information evolving into digital formats. While working at Georgia Tech he became fascinated with architecture and empathic design and has since aspired to create inspiring learning environments for students and faculty. Brian views each day as an experiment with the goal of constantly improving. His focus is now shifted to considering how librarians and library engagement can become more seamlessly integrated into the campus infrastructure and embedded across the entire learning enterprise.

Kenley Neufeld is the Dean of Educational Programs at Santa Barbara City College and also a mindfulness teacher in the Plum Village tradition of Thich Nhat

Hanh. Prior to serving as dean, Kenley was the Library Director at SBCC for eight years. Kenley loves playing with technology, experimenting with new ideas, and breaking down barriers. He says, "Being a library leader has been exciting because I have been able to support change and innovation in my library as well as the professional organizations I've worked with along the way." Kenley is a lifelong pacifist, a vegetarian, a music connoisseur, and has a passion for politics, reading, travel, and motorcycles. Kenley has been with his partner for 26 years and together, have two sweet children. The two public leaders who have inspired him the most have been Mahatma Gandhi and the Venerable Zen Master Thich Nhat Hanh.

Erin T. Smith has had the pleasure of working with the students, faculty, and staff of Westminster College in New Wilmington, Pennsylvania, for over a decade. She currently serves as the Associate Dean for Library and Information Services, where she has been hard at work developing a portfolio of elevator speeches that range from $100 to $1 million. She jokes, "I am occasionally terrified of getting stuck in an elevator with a donor and being so traumatized I forget all of them." But every day she marvels at her luck to be a library leader at a small liberal arts college when the changing technological landscape has opened up possibilities for her students and faculty that could not have been imagined in a print-based scholarly communication system.

Maureen Sullivan is a widely recognized leader and educator in the library profession. She has designed and presented a number of annual leadership development programs including the Texas Accelerated Library Leaders (TALL Texans) Institute, the New England Library Leadership Symposium (NELLS), and the Mountain Plains Leadership Institute. She is the 2012–13 president of the American Library Association (ALA). During her term, ALA created its first national leadership institute, Leading to the Future, and she worked with the Harvard Graduate School of Education to establish Library Leadership in a Digital Age. In 1999, during her term as president of the Association of College and Research Libraries, she helped to create the Leadership Institute for Academic Librarians at the Harvard Graduate School of Education.

Rosalind Tedford is the Director for Research and Instruction at the Z. Smith Reynolds Library at Wake Forest University. She earned her B.A. in English and Psychology as well as her M.A. in English from Wake Forest and an MLIS from the University of North Carolina at Greensboro. In addition to managing the research and instruction programs at Wake Forest, she teaches for-credit information literacy courses and is the liaison to the Politics and Psychology departments. She finds the unknowns of starting a big new project to be both the most exciting and terrifying aspects of leadership but loves being part of big conversations and big decisions both inside the library and out on campus. In her free time, she can be found with her two kids, attending plays, visiting Frank Lloyd Wright buildings, watching ACC basketball and reading. She admires many leaders for many things, but perhaps none more than Lynn Sutton, former Dean of the ZSR Library, for her transformative leadership and expert mentorship.

---- Preface ----

OUR CRUCIBLE MOMENTS

Our lives are composed of thousands of moments. Most slip by with little consequence or notice by others. For leaders, a single moment, perhaps just 60 seconds, can define the course of their leadership path, or in unfortunate cases, bring it to an end. Difficult as it may seem to believe, any crucible moment for leaders can serve as the test that becomes their pivotal swing toward success or failure. We see examples with some regularity. A politician publicly states something completely inappropriate or fails to respond to a situation that calls for strong leadership. A business executive has the opportunity to do good for the community but makes a bad decision that results in the exploitation of workers or customers. A little-known community leader stands up to an injustice and earns the trust and support of many followers. Some of these crucible events happen with high levels of media attention while others go mostly unnoticed.

Future generations of aspiring leaders will read about some of these crucible moments as case studies for learning to realize that almost any moment, even one that may seem mundane, has the capacity to test our leadership ability. Whether our response to the test is right or wrong, what is more crucial is how we emerge from it, what we learn, and how we use the experience to shape ourselves as leaders. While there is little we can do to prepare ourselves for crucible moments, we can work to develop the leadership qualities that will guide our actions so that we are hopefully ready when faced with a crucible moment. One way to develop the right qualities is to study and learn from the stories of leaders who have experienced crucible moments, survived them, and gone on to lead their organizations and colleagues to great achievements.

Where are these stories? One can often find them in business literature among the case studies of leaders, the ones who overcame the odds to achieve greatness as well as the ones who did get to the top but managed to fall from grace. We also find these stories about politicians, religious leaders, or even everyday people who rose above the odds to perform some great act of leadership. These stories should both influence and inspire us to be great leaders. But what about library leadership stories? Where are they found? The answer provides insight into the origins of the book *Crucible Moments*. Why do librarians need another book about leadership? Not only is there an endless stream of general literature about how to lead but there are many books that will help managers, leaders, and those who aspire to lead explore the mechanics of the kind of work and skills, including supervision, budgeting, and communication, that we typically associate with leadership.

Crucible Moments is a different kind of leadership book. It neither claims to teach the reader how to be a leader nor what leaders do. It is a book about why librarians become leaders and it offers the lessons of leadership through the stories of leaders at different phases of their careers. It is a book about the passion that motivates ordinary librarians, which is where we begin to choose the leadership path. Sometimes the choice is intentional but for some it comes as somewhat of an accident—or the result of a crucible moment. What the stories have in common are two things: inspiration and influence. Readers will be both inspired by the stories of these librarian leaders and will hopefully be encouraged to seek their own leadership path. Other leadership books can give librarians information about skills for leading library organizations. *Crucible Moments* gives librarians a reason and a purpose for choosing to lead. It does so by sharing the moments that forged librarians as leaders.

The stories start with my own tale of moving through a series of leadership positions but not really developing a passion for leadership and higher education until I found myself in the right position to be influenced by other leaders, and learned about leadership in a formal education program for future higher education leaders. No two library leaders are alike due to the different ways they come into positions of leadership. In my chapter I explain how my experience as a business librarian brought me into contact with leadership in the corporate world, and how that ignited my interest. It also made me more aware of librarians' general aversion to business. Thus, in the chapter, I encourage librarians to look to business for more stories about leadership, as well as encourage them to use those stories and the lessons learned to craft a personal mission statement that will help articulate a philosophy or outlook on what it means to be a leader and what differentiates us personally as leaders.

The first section is composed of two chapters on what it means to be a leader. These chapters differ slightly from the others in that what they communicate is not so much leadership stories but rather what aspiring and even current leaders need to be thinking about to establish themselves as leaders. The first is authored by a librarian who is synonymous with leadership, not only because of decades of strategic consulting and delivering leadership workshops, but also for "walking the walk" as the leader of librarianship's most prominent associations. In her chapter, Maureen Sullivan shares what leaders need to know to succeed in a VUCA (volatility, uncertainty, complexity, and ambiguity) world. By incorporating mindfulness, hope, and compassion into their practice, the library leaders can cope with crucible moments and turn their challenges into opportunities. Sullivan offers readers the leadership advice she has accumulated over a long career of teaching leaders to excel. Well-known educational technologist Joshua Kim completes the section with a chapter filled with ideas and advice for those who wish to lead in the tumultuous landscape of tomorrow's higher education institution. Kim brings a non-librarian's perspective to what it takes to lead in libraries with one foot in the past and the other in the future. For Kim, successful leadership is about adapting to change and driving libraries to be campus technology leaders when their institutions are facing greater competition with fewer resources. With his vast experience in the fast-paced world of educational technology, Kim's advice is perfect for leaders from any sphere of librarianship, where leading staff to leverage new technology to serve communities is a requisite skill.

The next section features library leaders who share their stories to inspire us to start from humble beginnings and follow our own path to leadership. It is said that three things impact a leader's chances for success: education, career experience, and behavior. Irene M. H. Herold is an expert on leadership programs, having written a doctoral dissertation about her studies of many library leadership development programs. She shares how her education and career experience influenced her leadership path and eventually led her to delve deeply into leadership development. A lifelong educator, Herold's career trajectory moves from middle school teacher to dean of a major research library. She relates how different people and events along the way influenced her career moves, taking advantage of opportunities along the way. One constant for Herold is the value of being a student of leadership, a practice she recommends to readers at all levels of leading.

While many of the chapters in *Crucible Moments* speak to the importance of mentors in shaping careers, Patrick Dawson offers the most in-depth discussion of how mentors influenced him, and, in turn, inspired him to lead at every opportunity. Through the story of his experience, Dawson covers how mentors impact aspiring leaders in both formal and informal relationships. He emphasizes the role of mentoring as a way to increase diversity in librarianship. Though he came to mentoring accidentally, Dawson makes it clear that librarians who want to lead should take advantage of mentors and give back to other aspiring leaders by mentoring them. Well-known for his leadership within many different library associations, Trevor A. Dawes is highly regarded among peers for his mentoring of newer-to-the-profession librarians. Dawes weaves a story that blends his knowledge of leadership theory and practice with the inside story of how he overcame his initial doubts about his ability to lead. Helped by a supportive family, caring coworkers, and library leaders who encouraged him to become professionally active, Dawes eventually finds his path to library leadership. The key to making it happen, shares Dawes, is having a leadership plan—a strategy that can help aspiring leaders by laying out a personal mission for leadership success.

Few of the leaders who contribute to *Crucible Moments* would be where they are now without the passion to lead and improve their libraries for the benefit of the community. The next section features two contributors whose passion for leading and taking risks to do so clearly emerges in their stories. Working primarily at only one institution, it was a passion for accepting new responsibilities and taking on tasks from which others shied away that put Rosalind Tedford on a tried and true path to leadership. Though she describes herself as a reluctant leader, Tedford demonstrates again and again how leadership happens everywhere in the library organization, not just in the administrative office. One of her finest observations is that crucible moments are both where we ourselves are shaped as leaders and where we learn to lead by observing how other leaders work their way through their crucibles. Aspiring library leaders often ask how one ascends to a significant leadership position in librarianship. In his chapter, Jon E. Cawthorne unravels some of those mysteries. It starts as a long journey, one that requires many hours of commitment to personal development and learning how to serve others. What nurtures Cawthorne through his long journey is his passion to explore the possibilities, learn from excellent mentors, and take advantage of opportunities to lead. No leader's development is complete without regular personal reflection, and this chapter inspires readers to believe they are capable of the same long journey, fueled by the kind of positive vision that sustained Cawthorne along the way.

One frustration for community college librarians is that books about leadership and management often tend to overlook the unique environment in which they work. *Crucible Moments* offers a section containing the leadership perspective from two librarians who are community college leaders: José Aguiñaga and Kenley Neufeld. Both share that their leadership happened within and outside the library at their institutions, primarily in a role as a leader among faculty with whom they experience labor solidarity. As a first-generation Latino who earns a doctoral degree, Aguiñaga establishes a challenging path for himself. What helps him succeed as a leader is pushing himself to lead in the library by taking on positions of increasing responsibility. He seeks leadership lessons throughout every phase of his career, whether it's learning to work with library product vendors, being professionally active as an association leader, or participating in shared governance. Aguiñaga's leadership story is largely about serving others, which he believes is the path to being a true collaborator. Another path to leadership starts by finding a space in which to excel in order to take others on difficult journeys of change. For Kenley Neufeld that space is information technology. His story is one of a diligent and lifelong pursuit of technology experimentation and learning, and it is a path that led Neufeld to the leadership fast track at a community college. However, it is a path with hurdles, because leading librarians through technology change is among the greatest of leadership challenges. Along the way, Neufeld discovers there is more to life than having a successful technology leadership role, and this pushes him to discover that mindfulness and spirituality are essential to his unique leadership style. Though he started out as an accidental leader, as did some of the other contributors, Neufeld is most intentional in his new role as a non-library academic administrator in a different yet related leadership path at this community college.

Not every leadership story fits into a neat category, and those from Char Booth, Brian Mathews, Erin Smith, and Eboni Johnson are less easy to fit into a neat container. Though they contain some elements of leadership stories about career paths taken, the contributors in this section offer unique insights into how they are intentional about wanting to lead, despite the fears and uncertainties that all leaders face. For Char Booth, leadership is something she does not come to naturally and in her chapter she is at her introspective best in reflecting on what leadership means to her. Char shares the four factors—conviction, vision, support, and elasticity—that enabled her to stop mishearing, suppressing, or questioning her own voice. For many leaders, as Char describes, becoming empowered to lead is a process of finding one's voice and articulating a vision in which others believe and support. Becoming a leader is less about the position and more about the project for Brian Mathews. His opportunities to lead are often characterized by becoming a member of the community and then making connections that lead to engagement with the library. That means being creative, innovative, and intentional about designing programs that meet the users where they are. Making progress often means contending with resistance, and readers can learn how Mathews managed to overcome this barrier, which leads to some engaging leadership stories. Leaders may learn best when things are kept simple, and that's what Erin Smith likes to do. Her leadership philosophy is to "start with a 'Yes.'" Her stories provide examples of how to do that by being intentional about getting to "yes" and making things happen even when the odds are against your success. Smith has few rules, other than no nudity, no fire, and good grammar. That means her methods involve some unorthodox approaches, but that is what it sometimes takes for great leaders to take a "yes" from start to finish. Facing our crucible moments requires courage and self-confidence. Eboni Johnson, in her chapter, likens this passage through the crucible as a process of navigating choppy waters. She reminds us that sometimes our failures become catalysts to help us achieve our potential as leaders. With the help of others and a belief in oneself, Johnson finds it is possible to move beyond self-doubt and the fear of failure to arrive at a point of smoother sailing, where she can be intentional about navigating her future leadership path.

Crucible Moments concludes with a gut-wrenching tale from Peter Bromberg that serves as a case study of a protracted crucible situation. For Bromberg, leadership is about one's ability to influence others to adopt a cause and follow a course of action. His chapter illustrates how taking on a personal mission to right a wrong requires leaders to harness all that they have learned about leadership in order to leverage their influence to mobilize people to take action. Using his training as an executive coach allowed Bromberg to adopt strategies that energized him through a difficult public dispute. What this case study has in common with many of the

other leadership stories is the self-discovery that our crucible moments are opportunities to learn and improve as leaders.

Being a leader involves making tough decisions and asking people to take on
challenging responsibilities. In that respect, serving as a book editor requires leadership skill. I asked these contributors to take on a difficult task and to complete
it on a tight deadline. Sharing a story seems like it should be easy, and a personal
story even easier. But the truth is that it can be rather difficult to choose what to
say and how to say it. For many librarians it would be far easier to write a scholarly
essay in which one could quote many sources or share the results of a research
study. To deliver on what makes this book special, in sharing stories about inspiration and influence, requires that these authors dig into their roots to relate what
they've learned about leadership in order to share their experiences and knowledge
with you. We all hope that *Crucible Moments* delivers a powerful, thought-provoking
learning experience for readers so that it will inspire and influence them to choose
and shape a future in which leadership is at the core of their library practice.

DEDICATION
Many thanks to all the leaders who laid the groundwork for this project—for their
inspiration, their influence, and helping me get through my crucible moments.

ACKNOWLEDGEMENTS
To Rolf Janke for taking a chance on me . . . for believing in my vision . . .
for encouraging me to pursue it.

Many thanks to Sara Tauber for keeping this project on the tracks—and
reminding me about the light at the end of the tunnel.

Thanks to the Mission Bell Media team, Leah Watson and Mary Jo Scibetta,
for their contributions, support, and help in bringing this project to fruition.

Special thanks to the 14 amazing colleagues who made this book possible.
When I asked, you said "yes" and that will always mean a great deal to me.

Steven J. Bell
Editor

—— 1 ——

THE POWER OF STORIES: LEARNING FROM LEADERS AND THEIR CRUCIBLE MOMENTS

Steven J. Bell

///////////// TOP TAKEAWAYS IN THIS CHAPTER

» No one may ask you to lead; you may need to grasp that opportunity

» Who is your leadership influencer?

» Leadership stories can inspire us and instill lessons of leadership

» Leaders learn from their crucible moments

» Dealing with adversity to business

» Craft a personal mission statement

A Leader in Crisis

Are leaders born or made? It's one of the most heavily debated questions in the scholarship of leadership. There may be those few individuals who are truly born to lead and whose circumstances facilitate their rise to leadership. For the rest of us, the path to leadership requires time to discover or to shape our ability to lead. That process often happens across a variety of experiences, including our education, careers, and personal achievements. Formal educational opportunities, such as leadership development programs, contribute to the process by which we learn to become a leader or obtain the exposure to leadership situations that may determine our desire to pursue positions of leadership.

In addition to the combination of factors that influence how we learn to be leaders, there are events over which we have little control that shift our destiny and alter our path to leadership. Talk to almost any leader about the story of their progression into leadership and it's likely to contain one or more irregular but highly stressful situations that contributed to their growth as a leader. At the time, that leader may have questioned their leadership ability and whether they were suited to lead. If we successfully navigate these situations, and it is often the case that mentors or trusted advisers help with their insight and guidance, it can dramatically influence our future capacity for remarkable leadership.

Even experienced leaders may find themselves in completely unknown territory when this happens. In the aftermath they may discover it provided a learning experience that may help when the next challenge arises. Leadership scholars refer to these events as crucible moments. Crucibles do play an important role in shaping many leaders. Whether they are born to it or learn to become one, all leaders can benefit from the crucible experience as it builds on and blends into all the other education, experience, and prior knowledge gained in leadership roles. Here is the story of one leader engaged in a difficult, unexpected, and potentially disastrous crisis situation.

In November 2014, *Rolling Stone* magazine published a story about a campus rape that sent shockwaves through higher education but also touched nerves in American society in ways that reports of sexual assault rarely had before. Sexual assault on college campuses was a building story in higher education but what *Rolling Stone* shared was particular disturbing. America, unfortunately, paid little attention to the problem of campus sexual assault, but a fraternity gang rape of a freshmen student grabbed headlines and led to stories across the media.

Talk to almost any leader about their progression into leadership and it's likely to contain a story that shares one or more irregular but highly stressful situations that contributed to their growth as a leader.

The University of Virginia was already on edge following the abduction and murder of a female student just weeks before *Rolling Stone*'s exposé. Now it found itself under attack from its own student body, as well as the media, accused of doing not only too little to address an outraged student body but quite possibly of accepting a culture of sexual violence perpetrated primarily by its fraternities. How would the university administration respond in the face of a crisis situation that required a strong response on multiple levels?

This new crisis would challenge university president Theresa Sullivan to deliver an appropriate response that would instill confidence and assure the university community that appropriate measures would be taken to investigate the allegations. Sullivan's initial response, however, was problematic. Having survived a threat to her presidency just two years earlier, Sullivan was no stranger to confronting crucible moments. By all accounts, Sullivan was a popular and effective leader. That was insufficient to satisfy a demanding board of trustees that believed the president was to blame for the university's failure to quickly adopt massive open online courses. After a short two-year tenure, the board had Sullivan resign. This led to a massive backlash from Sullivan's supporters on campus, and it eventually gave the board no choice but to reinstate Sullivan.

Given the outpouring of rage from the *Rolling Stone* article and accusations of a dangerous campus climate for women at the University of Virginia, the pressure was on Sullivan to deliver a strong show of leadership to bring calm to the campus. Unfortunately, her first letter of response to the campus was perceived as being defensive and vague as to how the administration would deal with the current climate of violence. Faculty responded angrily and demanded immediate action. Sullivan responded with a second letter that clearly outlined a strong response and identified new strategies. The first strategy was to suspend all fraternity activity, a controversial but forceful show of action. Coupled with other efforts to bring the community together in conversation, Sullivan was able to weather the storm. Though the *Rolling Stone* article turned out to be full of errors and was widely condemned for its shoddy journalism, the events that followed its publication set the stage for the leadership crisis that Sullivan had to confront. It is passage through such crucibles that forge great leaders.

Experiencing the Crucible

What makes you a leader? It could be having the opportunity to take responsibility for a specific project, perhaps one of your own design, in which case leading is also an opportunity to bring to fruition an individual vision. Even when asked to take charge of a library project by a supervisor, the individual in charge is the person who will either successfully complete the project or encounter obstacles that will lead to failure. He or she will likely have a team of colleagues assigned to the project, and the capacity to influence those members to engage and invest in the project is a measure, or possibly a test, of one's capacity to lead. In the library profession, leading from the middle is how many librarians get their first taste of leadership. Some are drawn to it naturally and thrive on inspiring colleagues to accomplish something greater than the sum of the parts. Others have no desire to step into a leadership role.

Then there is leading at another level, the one at which President Sullivan found herself when navigating her institution through a dramatic, intense, and sudden situation that tested her ability to bring the campus community together to forge a bond that would help move everyone forward and toward a positive outcome. Library leaders at every level will always be responsible for projects and bring them to a successful close, but there's also a level of leadership that places the leader in a crisis where one's abilities to maintain composure and influence others to follow a chosen path are sorely tested. That's the type of leadership that we may naturally wish to avoid, yet it also gives leaders the experience they need to grow and develop the confidence needed to do great things. Think of these events as crucible moments that define who we are as leaders and, in the eyes of followers, establish us as leaders. Many great leaders have experienced a crucible moment that has shaped their capacity to have the confidence to lead, whether it's commanding a room, sharing a vision, or leading people through a time of crisis.

Notable leadership expert Warren J. Bennis along with coauthor Robert J. Thomas first explored this phenomenon in their classic 2002 *Harvard Business Review* article "Crucibles of Leadership." Pointing to qualities such as adaptability, perseverance, and mental toughness, the article introduced the idea of the crucible as a method of explaining how leaders emerge. In a subsequent book, also titled *Crucibles of Leadership*, Thomas states that crucibles "are more like trials or tests that corner individuals and force them to answer questions about who they are and what is really important to them." Not just mere challenges, these crucibles have transformative power that can radically shift how an individual thinks and behaves. Presence is having the confidence to know that no matter how tough the going gets, you can get your team through it and lead your organization along the right path.

Business Then Leadership

At the start of my own career there were no aspirations to lead, hardly unexpected for a new librarian just a few years removed from undergraduate studies. While the one required course in library management at my LIS program provided an introduction to basics such as the difference between Theories X, Y, and Z, it did little to create much passion or appreciation for library leadership. What I did aspire to was a rewarding career as a reference librarian in an academic library. Unfortunately, I lacked some of the qualifications often sought by employers, such as a second subject master's degree. I eventually got there, but the path was far from direct. It required two stints in small, one-person libraries. It was the second one that made the difference, and not just in my library career but in my appreciation for learning about leadership though the world of business. Spending two years as the librarian for a multifaceted consulting organization introduced me to the world of business, not only providing hundreds of hours of online searching experience that sharpened my business research skills, but exposing me to the business literature for which I developed an appreciation. If you become a reader of the business literature, it's all but impossible not to gain exposure to the subdiscipline of leadership and management.

Moving on to a reference librarian position at the Lippincott Library of the University of Pennsylvania Wharton School created a more significant opportunity to become immersed in the world of business. While my subject responsibilities at this premier business library were in areas other than leadership and management, there were many opportunities to learn about the inner workings of business organizations from multiple perspectives. Having access to one of the great business library collections made a difference. Several years into this position, a staff vacancy created an opportunity to move up to an administrative position and I was encouraged to do so by the library administration. This is a fairly common way that frontline librarians make the transition into a leadership role. Some may decide it's not for them,

It was a great learning experience, but more than that it created a passion for learning about leadership through stories.

while others will thrive on it and set themselves on a course for a director position. In some ways I was more eager to satisfy the leadership team and not disappoint them by passing up the opportunity to adopt this new management role. It turned out to be the right decision for me.

While I had the support, I unfortunately lacked adequate managerial preparation for leading a small department in a library with a fairly strong collective bargaining unit while wrestling with some strong-willed personalities, which apparently led to the departure of the librarian I was replacing. While I faced my share of occasional small crises, as a middle manager I was able to largely avoid a serious crucible moment. Entering the university's management academy was only marginally helpful but it did provide a few concrete skills and a support network within the institution's managerial cohort. Still, it was a fairly limited role that rarely offered a chance to make an impact on the library's services to the community.

Inspiration Through Stories

While this experience intensified my interest in leadership and presented my first opportunity for management responsibility, it remains a secondary influence in my progression as a leader. Deciding to fill the open assistant director position at Lippincott Library of the Wharton School created more enthusiasm for taking on leadership responsibility and having a significant role in developing the policies and programs that would shape our library as it went through a physical and organizational restructuring process. I knew I needed to become more knowledgeable and skilled as a library and higher education leader. To further my knowledge of the role of higher education leadership, I enrolled in the graduate program in higher education administration at the University of Pennsylvania. It was a great learning experience, but more than that, it created a passion for learning about leadership through stories.

The department chair at the time was a recognized expert on and author of many books and articles on higher education organizations and planning. He served as a consultant to dozens of institutions and advised presidents and trustees. As an instructor, he injected his lectures with a seemingly infinite number of leadership stories that amplified almost any research studies or organizational theories we discussed in class. This experience allowed me to view learning about leadership differently. It demonstrated the importance of the underpinning theory upon which we may base our understanding of leadership, but it is the stories of leaders, both successes and failures, that help put that knowledge into the context of leading organizations and influencing colleagues and community members. I admired this educational leader for both his research expertise and teaching style. His talent for interweaving theory and practice influenced how I would go on to learn about leadership, analyze the administrative situations I would encounter, and become a true lifelong learner and thinker about the great challenge of leading organizations, associations, and specific projects.

Where the best of the chair's stories coalesced was during the required seminar on higher education leadership. There is perhaps no harder job than college or university president. It requires reporting to multiple constituencies, from trustee to student, and somehow pleasing them all on a multitude of complex issues. It's a round-the-clock responsibility that requires the ability to be as equally supportive of the women's field hockey team as you are of the debate squad. Our department chair knew many presidents personally. This enabled him to tell the story behind the stories in the textbooks. Through all of the books one could detect the many important themes of leadership, but perhaps the most important one for our instructor was the ability to bring vision to the institution and then align the forces to create a plan of action and bring it to fruition. To his way of thinking, there was nothing worse than a president who allowed his or her institution to drift aimlessly, settling for mediocrity.

It's no surprise that one of his most admired books, and he was a fairly prolific author, tells the story of a single college that rises from relative obscurity to national prominence. The book, *Transforming a College*, details how two decades of leadership at Elon College allowed the institution to ascend to excellence while others succumbed to budget crises and other ailments that derailed their plans. How was it possible? Great leaders with a commitment to a vision who inspired trustees, faculty, administrators, students, and their other stakeholders to strive to make that vision a reality. There were crises along the way. The president and trustees faced their own crucibles over decisions to increase enrollment, to embark on a risky campus expansion, and to convert to a university.

Ironically, despite his intimate knowledge of higher education leadership, due to change within the top leadership of the Graduate School of Education, he was asked to vacate his position as chair of the higher education administration program. Eventually he moved on to full-time consulting. Before his departure, though, he guided me in preparing for my doctoral exams, advising me as I started researching my dissertation, and encouraged me to become a library leader. Two years later, and with my doctorate completed, I fulfilled his vision for me by leaving the second-in-command position at one of the world's greatest business libraries to be the person in charge at a small, little-known library at a specialized college that aspired to transition to a small university. I felt wholly unprepared to take the reins of leadership, even at an operation smaller than the one I was leaving. The chasm between assistant director and director is wider than imaginable.

Learning From Crucibles

Some of the contributors to this book hold formal leadership positions as directors or deans of libraries. Others aspire to do so. And yet others, like me, have moved from director positions to other types of leadership roles. Advancing to a director or dean position is a decision many library leaders will consider at some point in their careers. Which path each of us chooses to take will depend on a mix of our inspirations, influences, and crucibles, but what ultimately prods librarians to go after that dean or director slot is vision. A mix of factors shapes a vision that emerges along with a desire to find an academic library where it can be brought to fruition. One thing that most of these leaders have in common is their crucibles, both the ones that enable them to gain leadership experience as well as those encountered as leaders.

I've had my own crucible moments. A few involve management decisions, such as complex human resource dilemmas that required some nerve-wracking dealings, but not all. A memorable crucible occurred during my first appearance on the library professional development program, Soaring to Excellence (STE). Developed at DuPage Community College, STE was a teleconference professional development program that was conducted live in a studio and broadcast via satellite to thousands of librarians. As an experienced conference speaker I was confident. What caught me off guard were the television studio setting and the high degree of struc-

> I felt wholly unprepared to take the reins of leadership, even at an operation smaller than the one I was leaving. The chasm between assistant director and director is wider than imaginable.

ture in the program. Then there was the other member of the show's guest panel who ambushed me with an unexpected scenario after two rehearsals. It was a mean-spirited attempt to embarrass me on a live show but I managed to turn it into a positive for the audience. It turned out all right, but it was unnerving at times, and I was surely relieved when it was over.

In the end I believed it was a good experience, and I learned from giving what I thought was a less than satisfactory performance. I went on to participate in four more episodes of STE, including a solo appearance. That crucible moment contributed to my ability to achieve greater presence in future presentations. I learned the value of immersing myself in the presentation experience and worrying less about getting everything just right. If I was myself, if I communicated the stories, and if I connected with the audience, I knew that it would go well and be a great experience for the audience—even if it was less than perfect. Those are the types of experiences that help to build presence across all the ways and at all the levels at which you may lead.

Librarians' Business Aversion

Having spent a dozen years in the business specialist sector of the profession, it still surprises me that many librarians are averse to business. More than a few librarians have expressed their displeasure with business to me over the years. It's easy to understand why many academic librarians reject the idea that reading business literature is good professional practice. Many come from humanities and social science backgrounds and obtain little exposure to the business world. They may come to the profession from the business world where a bad experience left them disenchanted and anti-business. There's no denying that the strong negative image of business, especially since the Great Recession of 2008, hardly compels individuals to look to it for leaders.

It is true that business is about profit making and libraries are the antithesis of that universe; our strongest value is free, unfettered, and equal access to information for all community members. Libraries and for-profit enterprises are of two different worlds, but there are some good reasons why librarians may want to develop an appreciation for business, particularly if they have an interest in leadership. For those who want to continuously improve as a "leadager," a leader who also manages, keeping up with the world of business is a real boon to learning, inspiration, and ideation. Librarians who pay attention to business are not selling out. It's about discovering new possibilities to improve the library experience through better leadership.

Here are a few reasons to explain why I advocate for librarians to be more open-minded about learning leadership from the world of business:

» Much of what we know about what works when it comes to leadership comes out of research conducted by business scholars. The work of Jim Collins, author of top-selling books such as *Good to Great*, is based on research into the performance of thousands of companies and studies of the strategies of and decisions made by their leaders. Through Collins's findings we learn the attributes of the leaders who really make a difference in their company's success. In fact, what Collins's research revealed is that leadership is so crucial to an organization's shift from good to great that he coined the phrase *Level 5 leader* to communicate that a certain kind of leader is the key ingredient in allowing a company to succeed. It's a leader who blends personal humility with professional intensity. Collins also wrote that while you need to have the right people on the bus, without a Level 5 leader driving the bus, it won't get far.

» The experts from whom we learn about leadership are often coming out of the world of business, both practitioners and educators. It's an arena with a fast pace, and new ideas often formulate in the business world in advance of other professional venues. Just as we learn from research on leading creative organizations, such as Linda Hill's, a Harvard Business School faculty member, we also learn from board-room experience. Consider Sheryl Sandberg's blockbuster book *Lean In,* a personal story about gender differences in business and how women can achieve their leadership goals. Good leadership stories can come from other arenas, such as government, health care, or education. However, a preponderance of the books and articles about leadership emerge from the world of business.

» More so than other sectors, there is hefty risk taking in business. That leads to all types of crucible situations, interesting stories, and lessons to learn. Consider two areas of leadership that are among the most difficult to master: decision making and change leadership. There are both huge successes and failures from which leaders can learn. However, if not for those talented business writers with the capacity to put these lessons into highly engaging and readable literature, those lessons would go unshared. Business writers like Chip and Dan Heath come to mind for a great example of books, articles, and videos about and for leaders at every level of their careers.

» Business provides leaders with ideas they can use to help develop their vision and to better know and understand which trends and technology changes are likely to impact our organizations. Consider how design is increasingly integrated into business. Five years ago design and user experience were rare topics of discussion in libraries, outside the context of computer interfaces. Business leaders were early adopters of using design principles and design philosophy to change the ways their organizations operate. What librarians have learned from the infusion of design into business has led to a much greater appreciation for the importance of design to both problem solving and developing great library experiences. Keep in mind that learning from business means that we examine the dark side as well. What's bad about business, be it greed, exploitation, or hostility, can also provide valuable lessons for leaders.

The librarian's aversion to business is understandable. One simple thing these librarians can do, if they seek to learn more about leadership, is to minimally expose themselves to leadership stories. A recommended starting point is the *New York Times* "Corner Office" column. Each week it profiles a leader who answers a set of questions about becoming a leader and which philosophies or practices define their leadership style. While most of the leaders profiled do come from the for-profit sector, there are occasional interviews with leaders from nonbusiness sectors. Each column is a mini-lesson in exploring leadership. From there, librarian leaders may be encouraged to delve into the primary sources of business news, such as the *Wall Street Journal*, *BusinessWeek*, or *Fortune*. Each regularly profiles business leaders, politicians, inventors, and others who share their stories of success and failure. It may also help to speak to a business librarian. Find out why he or she is passionate about business. Get to know a business leader in your community. Developing an appreciation for business need not mean a librarian is selling out the core values that define them as an information professional. It can simply be another way to commit to learning how to be the best possible library leader.

Your Personal Leadership Mission

We are told leaders need to have a vision that articulates or expresses a future direction for the organization. A well-designed vision should create passion among employees and influence their desire to help bring that vision to fruition. Perhaps even before leaders build that vision, they need to know themselves well and have a clear sense of why a particular vision is important to their organization and community. Good leaders need to be focused and consistent. This vision pushes them to achieve their goals in a way that followers can anticipate and on which they can count. Having a personal mission statement can help leaders stay true to this fundamental approach. All of the experiences that contribute to a leader's development and growth—their mentors, their crucibles, what they learn from their jobs—all contribute to the evolution of their personal mission statement.

Personal mission statements are designed less for specifics than for providing a sense of purpose that guides who you want to be and what you want to do. Think of them as the guideposts along the road. To my way of thinking, a mission statement is less about having a daily reminder or mantra and more about constructing a solid underpinning for longer-term career and personal goals. A mission statement is a touchstone that keeps us on the right path when we encounter a difficult choice or a disappointing setback. It may help you decide when to say "no." Your statement will act as your personal gyroscope to keep you upright in times of instability.

Developing your mission statement may come to you in a bolt when you least expect it or it might take weeks or months. There's no rush. It may help to think about your WHY. That's a reference to Simon Sinek's inspirational book *Start With Why*. Sinek's point is that successful leaders and organizations, the ones that make a difference, can easily articulate the WHY that defines their cause, purpose, and core beliefs. It may help you to gain a better sense of who you are and what you stand for, and, as Sinek would say, if you don't know what it is then you can't expect others to follow your lead. My WHY evolved into "things I can do to help academic librarians become better at advancing themselves and improving their libraries"—something I believe. It manifested itself in my efforts to write and present with a different and unique style (the HOW), and that translated into more meaningful tangible results (the WHAT). The ability to understand and articulate my personal WHY contributed to my personal mission statement. It may also work for you.

Once you have your statement you may wonder if it will need revision as your professional and personal status changes. Does your library's mission statement change? It usually does, as the needs of the community shift, as our technological capabilities grow, and as the priorities of the staff evolve. Personal mission statements may need to change as well, particularly when moving into leadership positions and the ends we aspire to achieve take on new meaning. What about my own mission statement? With a good sense of what I want to accomplish in my career, through my library work, professional commitments, writing and speaking, and aspirations for leading others, a more timely statement is appropriate. I sought to keep it simple:

Think different. Be different. Make a difference.

What does that mean to me? Avoid trying to do what everyone else does. Avoid writing about what everyone else is covering. Avoid getting pigeonholed into one specialization. Try different ideas and possibilities. Look for new ways to make the library work better for the community. Stay focused on putting energy into actions that will make a difference. Some refer to the personal mission as the "inside-out strategy." Personal beliefs and ideas are at the core. It defines your purpose. Once you have your personal mission it will likely define your personal leadership story.

////////////// **REFLECTIONS: KEY LESSONS FOR LEADERS**

» Embrace your crucibles and learn from them
» Mentors can be a valuable source of leadership stories
» Overcoming an aversion to business can lead to more learning about leadership
» Vision is important but so is your personal leadership mission
» Craft a personal mission statement

References

Keller, George. *Transforming a College: The Story of a Little-Known College's Strategic Rise to National Prominence*. Baltimore, MD: Johns Hopkins University Press, 2004.

Rubin Erderly, Sabrina. "A Rape on Campus: A Brutal Assault and Struggle for Justice at UVA." *Rolling Stone* (November 19, 2014). http://www.rollingstone.com/culture/features/a-rape-on-campus-20141119.

Stripling, Jack. "Teresa Sullivan Will Step Down as UVa's President After Two Years in Office." *Chronicle of Higher Education* (June 10, 2012). http://chronicle.com/article/Teresa-Sullivan-Abruptly/132205.

Thomason, Andy. "How UVa's President Changed Her Tune on Sexual Assault." *Chronicle of Higher Education* (November 24, 2014). http://chronicle.com/blogs/ticker/how-uvas-president-changed-her-tune-on-sexual-assault/90153.

NOTE: The section on personal mission statements is adapted from my "Leading From the Library" column in *Library Journal*, dated December 3, 2014, originally written with the closing section of this chapter in mind. Retrieved from http://lj.libraryjournal.com/2014/12/opinion/leading-from-the-library/whats-your-personal-mission-leading-from-the-library-2.

—— 2 ——

TRANSFORMING LIBRARIES:
CHALLENGES, OPPORTUNITIES, AND PATHWAYS

Maureen Sullivan

///////////// TOP TAKEAWAYS IN THIS CHAPTER

» Challenges can be reframed to be opportunities

» Crucible experiences are an important source of leadership development

» Anyone can be a leader; managers must be leaders to be effective in today's libraries

» Leadership is a set of practices and competencies that can be learned

» Reframing a situation by learning to view it through different lenses leads to improved leadership practice

Reframing Challenges to Create Opportunities

Leaders in today's libraries face a number of serious and complex challenges inside the organization and in the larger world outside. The term *VUCA* is often used to describe the context in which leadership occurs today. "VUCA" represents four key characteristics—volatility, uncertainty, complexity, and ambiguity. This aptly captures the environment for library leadership today. These leaders face many challenges, a number of which are complex and represent situations with which the leader has little or no prior experience. Effective leaders learn to face challenges and often discover that reframing the challenge to be an opportunity is a very effective practice. Effective leaders also commit to the pursuit of personal mastery. They recognize that becoming an effective leader is a journey, one in which learning and the development of competence occurs as a result of experience. This experience is enriched when the leader takes time to reflect upon what has occurred and

Effective leaders learn to face challenges and often discover that reframing the challenge to be an opportunity is a very effective practice.

to identify ways to improve. There are many leadership theories, models, and resources available today to support this work. This article identifies several that are particularly useful for librarians in their practice of academic leadership.

Effective leadership is a relationship of reciprocity and mutual influence, one in which there is mutual trust and confidence between the leader and followers. This trust and confidence comes from interpersonal relationships in which there is direct, open, and honest communication. The leader recognizes and truly values the distinctive interests, competencies, work styles, and talents of followers. The leader appreciates and optimizes the individual differences among followers and expects each to deliver his or her best performance.

Daniel Goleman, in his 2013 *Harvard Business Review* article "The Focused Leader," used the framework of three key arenas—Self, Others, and the Wider World—to describe how and where leaders should focus attention to be effective. This model of three areas of attention for leadership effectiveness is a very effective means for continuous attention to leadership development. The first, "Self," includes being attuned to the full range of your emotions, developing a coherent understanding of your authentic self, and mastering self-control. The second focuses on having empathy and displaying empathic concern for "Others," and the third addresses the important need to turn attention outward and focus on the larger "Wider World" beyond self, others, and organization to understand trends, developments, and events. This area includes the leader's ability to focus on strategy, to foster innovation, and to practice systems thinking—an ability to understand the dynamics and interdependencies of organizational and larger systems.

Earlier, Goleman collaborated with Richard Boyatzis and Annie McKee to explore how emotional intelligence and its set of competencies correlated with leadership. In *Resonant Leadership* they describe the major areas of Mindfulness, Hope, and Compassion to be the key components of the practice of resonant leadership. They define this concept of leadership to be a relationship.

Resonant leaders are in tune with those around them. This results in people working in sync with each other, in tune with each others' thoughts (what to do) and emotions (why to do it). Leaders who can create resonance are people who either intuitively understand or have worked hard to develop emotional intelligence—namely, the competencies of self-awareness, self-management, social awareness, and relationship management. They act with mental clarity, not simply following a whim or an impulse.

Mindfulness is the capacity to be fully aware of all that one experiences *inside the self*—body, mind, heart, spirit—and to pay full attention to what is happening *around us*—people, the natural world, our surroundings, and events. **Hope** is an emotional state in which we feel elated about a future that seems feasible. It is accompanied by clear thoughts about what the future can be and how to get there. Leaders who demonstrate hope have dreams and aspirations and are in touch with those around them; they are optimistic and believe in their ability to make change; and they see the desired future to be realistic and feasible. **Compassion** is empathy and caring in action. The three components of compassion are understanding and empathy for the feelings and experiences of others, caring for others, and the willingness to act on those feelings of care and empathy.

Resonant leadership is a very useful framework for understanding how to create strong relationships with followers. Library leaders can use this framework to clarify and identify areas for their own development. As library leaders continue to face new and more complex challenges, the need for trust, confidence, and resonance in their relationships with followers and colleagues is essential.

The Challenges Leaders Face

Among the challenges today's academic leaders face are keeping up with the pace and complexity of technological change; having the resources necessary to support ongoing operations and to enable innovation and the pursuit of new initiatives; understanding and effectively responding to the changing needs, learning styles, and preferences of students, faculty, and scholars; being an effective contributor in the academy and providing the managerial leadership needed inside the library organization; engaging staff and other stakeholders in the creation of a compelling strategic plan and ensuring that daily operations are efficient and productive; focusing on day-to-day work performance results and giving time to strategic thinking and planning for the future; balancing work, career, and professional responsibilities; planning and leading transformational change; empowering staff and ensuring the commitment necessary for staff to act appropriately on this empowerment; transforming services, programs, and work processes and maintaining the quality of day-to-day performance; fostering an organizational climate of high performance, work satisfaction, diversity, inclusion, and innovation; encouraging staff to shift from a "fixed" mind-set to a "growth" mind-set; and making all of the changes necessary to develop an organization that will succeed and thrive in an increasingly digital world.

Every challenge presents an opportunity to think and act differently. In his chapter Steven Bell introduces the "crucible experience" as a set of circumstances that describe complex and difficult situations that test a leader's capacity to be effective. Crucible experiences are transformative in that they lead to significant changes in the way leaders think and behave. They stimulate learning and are significant experiences in leadership development. These crucible experiences also point to another set of challenges—those that arise from within the leader. These challenges can be framed as a set of dilemmas and include developing the capacity to be effective in both the management process and in providing leadership to a diverse group of followers; giving appropriate attention to developing oneself and to developing others; empowering others and determining when to use authoritative or consultative approaches to ensure effective and timely decision making; delegating work to others to support and encourage their learning and development; and determining the best use of one's own time, energy, and attention.

Keeping up with the pace and complexity of technological change; having the resources necessary to support ongoing operations and to enable innovation and the pursuit of new initiatives; understanding and effectively responding to the changing needs, learning styles, and preferences.

Managerial leaders in today's organizations also face the challenge of leading from the middle. They report to a more senior position in the organizational hierarchy and they have a series of positions and incumbents who report to them. Joan V. Gallos offered a compelling discussion of this position in her article, "The Dean's Squeeze: The Myths and Realities of Academic Leadership in the Middle," published in *Academy of Management Learning and Education* (December 2002). In 2011, Gallos and Lee G. Bolman produced *Reframing Academic Leadership* in which they addressed "understanding administrative life in the middle." They advocate that "college and university leaders face an important opportunity to use their positions in the middle of things to facilitate relationships and to bring the divergent needs of different parties together in support of institutional advancement." Leaders in academic libraries face the challenges that Gallos and Bolman describe and can reframe these challenges to be opportunities.

In their book, Gallos and Bolman offer an extensive discussion of the importance of reframing challenges to be opportunities. The process and strategies for doing this are based upon the four frames of leadership that Bolman developed with Terrence E. Deal. Their book, *Reframing Organizations: Artistry, Choice, and Leadership*, presents a thorough description of the four-frame model—structural, human resource, political, and symbolic—and provides a set of practical ways to use the frames to analyze organizational situations. Adopting a new mind-set, one in which the leader seeks to reframe a challenge to be an opportunity, is a critical step on the path to effective and rewarding leadership in libraries today. Learning to use the four-frame model is an important tool for reframing situations to enable more effective leadership practice.

Making the Most of Opportunities

Ron Heifetz, with his colleagues Alexander Grashow and Marty Linsky, promotes the practice of *adaptive leadership* as the most effective approach to managing and leading in challenging times. In their article "Leadership in a (Permanent) Crisis," (Harvard Business Review, July–August 2009) they define *adaptive leadership* as "the practice of mobilizing people to tackle tough challenges and thrive." It is "a daily opportunity to mobilize the resources of people to thrive in a changing and challenging world." They suggest that the choice is to "hunker down or press reset" and describe a set of leadership practices and strategies that have particular relevance and application in today's libraries. The four leadership practices are the following:

» Fostering adaptation
» Embracing disequilibrium
» Generating leadership
» Taking care of oneself

Each focuses on a domain of critical importance to leadership in academic libraries today.

Fostering adaptation is the practice in which leaders address the need to transform the work and the context in which that work is performed. It includes three major activities: confronting loyalty to legacy practices, distinguishing the work that is "essential" from the work that is "expendable," and "running numerous experiments." This calls for a new mind-set about the work, one in which leaders create a work environment that encourages a willingness to try new approaches in what Walter Shewhart called for in the 1920s: "Plan-Do-Check-Act."

Embracing disequilibrium focuses on creating a work environment in which staff accept the disruption that results from continuous change and learn to work well in this climate. Leaders reframe the disturbance that results from change so that it leads to "productive rather than destructive" responses. The key activities in this area are (1) monitoring the "thermostat" to ensure an appropriate level of disequilibrium, that is, generating enough heat for productivity and progress, but not so much that people experience burnout, or too little so that they are complacent and not fully engaged; (2) depersonalizing conflict by encouraging a focus on the issues or situation to be addressed or resolved; and (3) creating a "culture of courageous conversations," one in which individuals freely share their thoughts, ideas, and perspectives without fear. This calls for transparency and the "culture of candor" that Warren Bennis and James O'Toole describe in "What's Needed Next: A Culture of Candor" in the June 2009 issue of the *Harvard Business Review*.

Leaders "generate leadership" in their organizations by empowering staff to engage in adaptive work, by distributing leadership responsibility across the organization, by mobilizing everyone to generate solutions, and by actively leveraging the diversity that exists within and among the various individuals in the organization.

One distinctive and very important component of adaptive leadership is the fourth area of "taking care of yourself." This area of practice includes being both optimistic and realistic, finding sanctuaries (places where the leader can be reflective and regain perspective), reaching out to confidants to debrief and review actions taken and decisions made, bringing more of one's emotional self to the workplace (acting in an authentic and genuine way), and not losing oneself in the role and work to be performed.

Practicing the four components of adaptive leadership, recognizing the opportunities inherent in "leading from the middle," learning to use Bolman and Deal's four frames, and developing the ability to reframe challenges as opportunities are critical in being an effective leader in today's library organizations. They provide a foundation for leading from a strong and confident position to meet challenges by reframing them to be opportunities.

Pathways to Improving Leadership Practice

My 30-plus years of experience designing, conducting, and teaching a variety of leadership development institutes and programs have identified a series of activities and paths to be followed in a personal journey to become a more effective leader. There are a number of ways to embark upon and continue this journey. The following suggested pathways are also a means for library leaders to be more ready and able to turn challenges into opportunities.

Commit to continuous learning and your leadership development. Adopt a "growth" mind-set as described by Carol Dweck in "Mindset." Know your strengths and build upon them. Focus on what you do well. Take time to clarify your strengths. A very good resource for this work is *Strengths Finder for Leaders.* Every copy of this book contains a process and a code for completing a self-assessment to begin your work. Identify areas for your development. Do this based upon an assessment of what your situation requires and what you know about your current strengths. Seek opportunities to work with colleagues who bring complementary skills and abilities.

Believe in "The Ten Truths About Leadership" as set forth by James Kouzes and Barry Posner in *The Truth About Leadership*:

1. You make a difference.
2. Credibility is the foundation of leadership.
3. Values drive commitment.
4. Focusing on the future sets leaders apart.
5. You can't do it alone.
6. Trust rules, personal credibility, the cohesiveness and effectiveness of a team, and the organization's performance.
7. Challenge is the crucible for greatness.
8. You either lead by example or you don't lead at all.
9. The best leaders are the best learners.
10. Leadership is an affair of the heart.

Seek support for your learning and development from a variety of sources. Invite others to offer comments and provide constructive feedback. Seek this information from a variety of trusted sources. Listen carefully to understand and to learn. Avoid responding right away, especially in a defensive way. Take time to reflect and carefully consider what steps you might take.

Practice the skill of active listening. Give full attention to what others say and listen carefully for the key messages. Be careful to put aside your own thoughts and focus on what is being said. Listen with an open mind and avoid judging too soon what others have to say.

Prepare a learning and development plan. Set goals for what you want to learn. Create an action plan to achieve these goals. Clarify your learning preferences. Pursue learning activities that match these preferences. Be open to new ones, too. Identify role models, others from whom you can learn. One very good way to prepare for this is to reflect on the following set of questions as posed by Peter Drucker in "Managing Oneself," an article first published in the March–April 1999 issue of the *Harvard Business Review*.

>> **What are my strengths?** What do you do well? Where do you achieve your best results?

>> **How do I perform?** How do you approach your work? What is your preferred work style?

>> **How do you learn?** What methods work best for you (reading, lecture, watching others, through experience, etc.)?

>> **Do you work well with others?** Are there relationships that need to improve?

>> **What are my values?** What are your core values? What do you most cherish in your life and in your work? Are there any conflicts between your personal values and the organizational values of your library?

>> **Where do I belong?** Do you belong where you are now? Is there something you would rather do?

>> **What should I contribute?** What does the situation require? Given your strengths, your way of performing, and your values, how can you make the greatest contribution to what needs to be done? What results are necessary to make a difference? What do you need to do?

>> **How can I improve my relationships with others?** What steps can you take? What skills might you need to develop?

Practice mindfulness, the art of living in a state of full, conscious awareness of yourself, others, and the context in which you work and live. Remain aware and attentive to your own thoughts and emotions, to what others say and do, and to events and developments in your surroundings. Engage in reflective practice. Take time to review what you have experienced to identify what you may have learned. Consider what sense you can make of these experiences and what this might suggest for your leadership development.

Identify ways to be aware of trends, developments, and significant events that are likely to affect your work, your career, and your professional life. Remain attuned to trends and developments that will have significant influence on the future of libraries and librarianship. One recent and very useful resource to consult is the Center for the Future of Libraries section of the American Library Association's Web site, www.ala.org. The center's founding director has identified about 20 major trends for which he has provided a full description of each on the site. He updates this information on a regular basis.

Study the Bolman and Deal four frames to understand them and then develop the capacity to use all of them in a given situation. Know your preferred frame. Read the Bolman and Gallos book, *Reframing Academic Leadership,* for practical and timely guidance on the application of the frames and how to lead from the middle.

Look for opportunities to help others learn. Teaching others is often the best way to reinforce one's own learning. This includes regular attention to work activities that can be delegated to others to encourage their growth and development.

Invite a colleague to be your learning partner. Coach and support each other. Turn to one another for guidance. Serve as each other's sanctuaries.

Be aware that learning includes "unlearning" old habits and practices. Be patient with yourself through this process. Carefully select areas to develop and make a firm commitment to this work. Focus on your strengths and what you do well. Plan your development from this platform. Seek feedback from a variety of trusted sources.

Adopt a positive attitude toward learning and change—for yourself, your colleagues, and the organization. See the organization and your work as a laboratory for learning. Accept that your learning is a way of being in your work and in your career. View learning as a lifelong process and make a personal commitment to be responsible for your own learning and development.

Recognize the different stages in leadership development. Warren Bennis offers one model in his article, "The Seven Ages of the Leader," published in the January 2004 issue of the *Harvard Business Review.* View your leadership practice to be a journey, one in which you will learn and grow from experience. Seek continuous improvement and growth, not perfection on this journey.

Develop and use a set of coping strategies and stress management techniques that work for you. Become knowledgeable about the stress response and know what your stress triggers are. Identify a range of possibilities: exercise, meditation, mindfulness, and relaxation techniques. Take a systematic approach to solving problems and develop action plans that are achievable. Develop a support network.

Take risks and encourage risk taking in others. Foster an attitude of experimentation in the workplace. Provide incentives and rewards for this behavior. Develop your skills in effective decision making and help others to learn these skills. Know your propensity for taking risks and the conditions under which you are more likely to do so. Recognize that risk taking involves making decisions to pursue goals under conditions of uncertainty with the possibility of loss as well as gain. Take time to think the situation through. Do a gains and losses assessment. Identify some ways to reduce the uncertainty. Develop an action plan.

Develop your vision and invite others to clarify theirs, then create a shared vision of an aspirational future. Create a compelling narrative of the future. Learn how to convey this to others through the use of possible scenarios and metaphors. Develop and tell stories that will inspire and motivate others.

Believe in possibilities. When leaders focus on the future and possibilities, followers are more likely to do so, too. Be optimistic and encourage others to find the opportunities in the challenges and to have a positive outlook.

Accept the strengths and individual differences of others. Take time to get to know others, their interests, preferred styles for working in groups and teams, communicating, solving problems, and performing their own work. Believe in the capacity and potential of others. Accept others for who they are.

Strengthen your capacity to have empathy and understanding for others. Learn and practice the "empathy triad" as set forth by Goleman in "The Focused Leader." This triad is comprised of three distinct areas of empathy—cognitive, emotional, and empathic concern.

Coach and develop others to reach their potential. Approach this work from the perspective of a guide, one who helps the other to clarify the situation, to explore options, and to reinforce the responsibility of the individual to assume accountability for acting to resolve the situation.

Be open, honest, and direct in communication with others. Tell the truth even when it is difficult to do so. Encourage others to do the same. Make every effort to create a culture of candor in your organization.

Expect high performance and strong commitment. Carefully communicate performance expectations and hold others accountable for meeting them.

Invite them to prepare their own action plans for accomplishing their work and developing their competence.

Empower individuals to make decisions. Determine what needs to be accomplished and enable others to decide how they will do this. Provide positive reinforcement. Recognize that the shift to empowerment requires deep learning and takes time and experience.

Focus on leadership development as a key initiative within the library. Make it a clear priority. Create a program of activities for staff and align the learning objectives with the larger change initiatives and goals of the library. Identify meaningful and challenging assignments and projects. Offer the opportunity to participate to a broad group of individuals. Assume that everyone has the potential to contribute and act on this. Establish a mentoring program. Take steps to create a learning culture, one that expects, fosters, and supports innovation.

Take a broad view of who will have the ability to lead. Be careful not to prejudge potential too early. Create opportunities for potential leaders to interact with effective, more experienced leaders.

Ensure that the current formal leaders in the library are held accountable for effective leadership. Insist that their leadership practice matches the espoused leadership philosophy and values of the library. Remain alert to complex and challenging situations. Put managers and potential leaders in those situations.

Practice systems thinking, the habit of thinking at the macro level and seeing the organization as a set of dynamic and interdependent interactions. Follow Ron Heifetz's admonition to "step up to the balcony" and be above the "dance floor" to gain a broader perspective and see a situation differently.

Pay attention to the wider, external world. Identify those trends, developments and events that are likely to affect the library, the profession and the work of librarians. Deliberately turn outward to understand the larger context in which the library exists. Pay attention to the changes in our world and then adapt. Develop strategies to position the library to thrive in the ever-evolving digital world.

Strive to be a focused, adaptive leader who engages others in the innovative, meaningful work that is so essential to fulfilling the continuing mission of the library to make a difference in student learning, faculty teaching, research, and scholarship as the world in which the work is accomplished evolves and brings new challenges and opportunities. Be the leader who inspires an optimistic and energetic focus on excellence and accomplishment.

REFLECTIONS: KEY LESSONS FOR LEADERS

» Successful leaders continue to develop their capacity to do their best work

» Leadership is a journey of challenges and opportunities

» Effective leaders work with others to transform challenges into opportunities

» Leaders must take care of themselves

» Leaders must focus on what is most important—this is a critical ability

References

Bennis, Warren, Daniel Goleman, and James O'Toole. *Transparency: How Leaders Create a Culture of Candor*. San Francisco: Jossey-Bass, 2008.

Bolman, Lee G., and Terrence E. Deal. *Reframing Organizations: Artistry, Choice, and Leadership*. 5th ed. San Franscico: Jossey-Bass, 2013.

Bolman, Lee G., and Joan V. Gallos. *Reframing Academic Leadership*. San Francisco: Jossey-Bass, 2011.

Dweck, Carol. *Mindset: The New Psychology of Success*. New York: Random House, 2007.

Goleman, Daniel. "The Focused Leader: How Effective Executives Direct Their Own—and Their Organizations' Attention." *Harvard Business Review* (December 2013).

Kouzes, James M., and Barry Z. Posner. *The Truth About Leadership: The No-Fads, Heart-of-the-Matter Facts You Need to Know*. San Francisco: Jossey-Bass, 2010.

Rath, Tom, and Barry Conchie. *Strengths-Based Leadership: Great Leaders, Teams and Why People Follow*. New York: Gallup Press, 2008.

3

LEADING NON-INCREMENTAL CHANGE IN THE ACADEMIC LIBRARY: ONE VIEW FROM OUTSIDE YOUR PROFESSION

Joshua Kim

///////////////// TOP TAKEAWAYS IN THIS CHAPTER

» Competitive forces are pushing rapid and often destabilizing change across higher education

» Academic librarians who wish to ascend to leadership roles will need to commit to leading non-incremental change

» Learning is emerging as a key institutional differentiator, and academic librarians are well positioned to participate in and lead innovation efforts around learning

This is a book about learning with library leadership. It is in the title. I am not a library leader. If you're looking for answers, or at least ideas and stories, to help guide you in your own library leadership path, I suggest you read the other chapters. My goal is to convince you that you're essential in leading nonincremental change at your college or university. The reasons that you're an essential change leader are twofold:

1. Our colleges and universities need to change.
2. You need to be part of leading that change.

My hypothesis is that the path to academic library leadership is changing. Leadership is now less about management and more about building coalitions and gathering resources in support of a vision of the future. The job of

Experimentation, risk taking, and decision-making based on data (rather than intuition) will define most of our work for the years to come.

an academic leader, including an academic library leader, is to clearly, forcefully, and consistently articulate this vision for the future. Effective leaders will closely align this vision with the core goals of the their academic institutions, and will be able to communicate this vision in a way that resonates deeply with a broad range of stakeholders.

To be clear, the academic leader (and the academic library leader) is not only or always the person in a recognized leadership role. Now more than ever, leadership needs to emerge from every position in the academic (and academic library) hierarchy. Effective leadership from the middle will be the essential ingredient if our institutions are going to overcome the inertia of the status quo. The importance of leading from the middle is that those are the very people who interact on a daily basis with students, faculty, and staff.

The complexity of changes necessary to meet the challenges of higher education in the 21st century are too great for any single college president or library dean to either fully understand or direct. Authority, discretion, and decision-making power will be pushed to the edges of the organization. Experimentation, risk taking, and decision making based on data (rather than intuition) will define most of our work for the years to come. Those best able to thrive in the new academic environment will need to be comfortable with ambiguity and gray areas. Established methods and proven operations will be less helpful in a rapidly changing environment. Organizational structures will be fluid, and many of us will feel as if we are living through a never-ending reorganization. Decisions will need to be made at a faster pace than is traditionally possible with a structure that stresses consensus building. The traditional roles of managers and subordinates will be challenged as organizations flatten out in order to provide better service and more nimble operations.

An Outsider's View

Before we dive into why I believe that tomorrow's academic library leader will need to prioritize nonincremental change, I'd like to share a little bit about my background—and how I came to be connected with the academic library community. The first thing that you should know about me is that I go to work everyday in an academic library. My office in the Baker Library at Dartmouth is directly off the main hall that once housed our card catalog. When it was built in 1928, the Baker Library held 240,000 volumes but was big enough to hold half a million. There's a door in my office that leads directly into the Class of 1902 reading room.

Professionally, I am embedded (in a very physical sense) in the academic library. The history, the present, and the future of the academic library caress my senses every hour that I am on campus. My work as Dartmouth's director of digital learning initiatives brings me in constant contact with academic library professionals. I work with librarians on formulating strategy for our investments and projects in learning innovation. I work with librarians as team members in developing and running new online and low-residence degree and nondegree programs. I work with librarians in our efforts to figure out how to provide research and information services to an increasingly geographically distributed and mobile group of learners. Almost everything that we do in digital learning now involves a librarian, a library service, or a library resource.

My job is within our Dartmouth Center for the Advancement of Learning, known as DCAL, a center that is also housed within—but does not organizationally sit under—our academic library. Yet, despite my physical proximity within an academic library and my close collaboration with library professionals, I am an academic library outsider. I am not a member of the academic library tribe. My people are generally thought of as educational technologists, instructional designers, and those working in teaching and learning centers. I work in your building, I hang out with your practitioners, but I am not one of you. I don't speak your language, I don't go to your meetings. I observe, but am not a member of, your culture. Each day of work within an academic library feels like a visit to a foreign country. A familiar country where I can hold a conversation and find my way around, but one in which I am constantly discovering differences in culture, orientation, and outlook from the place from which I came. I am an immigrant in the academic library. Your ways seem mysterious and exotic. Your people are warm, inviting, and friendly. But I remain a library expatriate. This vantage point offers me a unique view of library leadership.

Leading in a Time of Resource Scarcity

The question of how our colleges and universities will evolve is intimately tied up with how the higher education industry will change as a whole. If we were ever cloistered islands of scholarship and learning, those days have long ended. Anyone who seeks to move into a leadership role in higher education, be that role in the academic library, in the technology units, or in central administration, needs to come to grips with three realities:

> **Reality 1:** Our higher education industry is increasingly competitive, with industry-wide change and disruption set to accelerate in the years to come.
>
> **Reality 2:** A scarcity of resources, be that resource money, people, or time, is the new normal at every college and university.
>
> **Reality 3:** Any successful academic leader will need to envision and lead nonincremental change.

Most of us chose a life in higher education because we wanted our work to match our values. We became academics (a category that includes librarians and learning technologists, as well as professors) because we believe in the educational and knowledge-producing mission of academy. As we move into leadership roles, however, we quickly realize that fulfilling this mission is not possible without resources. We start to understand that much of our job as academic leaders is to manage within resource scarcity, and to make the case for more resources for the organizations that we lead. As we ascend to greater levels of responsibility, our obligations to our colleagues throughout the organization increase. The best academic leaders understand that their job is to enable and support the work of those on the front lines of the organization's operations and services. As leaders perform less hands-on service and patron-facing operations, they expend more effort working to create an environment where those working in the organization can do their best work.

The old path to academic leadership was incremental. We gained increasing responsibility as we moved into positions that managed more people and a bigger budget. We worked to sustain consistent levels of service, while constantly seeking out ways that our operations and methods could evolve. We honed our managerial techniques, built strong networks with leaders and emerging leaders within and outside of out institutions, and did whatever we could to contribute to the productivity and efficiency of our libraries, departments, units, and divisions.

Today, the successful academic leader—and in particular the successful academic library leader—will need to throw this old model of leadership progression out the window. Steady-state evolution in an environment of rapid dislocation and change will not be enough. The academy, including the academic library, needs to find ways to make some big changes. We need to figure out how we can absorb, and even encourage, risk taking and experimentation.

Why is this? The reason, as with most things in life, comes down to money. With the exception of a few very rare cases, the fundamental economic model that we relied on to pay for higher education (including the academic library) is breaking down. The public disinvestment in higher education is real. The public sector is running away as fast as it can from funding our public institutions of higher learning. Costs have been shifted to the student (and their parents) in the form of higher tuition and fees, but these costs can only go up so much. At the same time that public institutions are figuring out how to manage without public support, private tuition-dependent institutions are also dealing with financial challenges.

A combination of shifting demographics (aging, migration, lower fertility), long-term economic trends (the hollowing out of the middle class), and increased costs are driving the big financial challenges faced by almost every school. Costs are up, yields are down, and the discount rate needed to entice tuition-paying students keeps going up. As revenues decline, the costs of running our colleges and universities are also going up. Technology, rather than drive costs down, has only increased the demands on our services. What academic library is not a 24/7/365 academic library now—at least digitally if not physically? Every other cost, from health care to building maintenance, is also going up. The academic library, and tomorrow's

The best academic leaders understand that their job is to enable and support the work of those on the front lines of the organization's operations and services.

academic library leaders, will find themselves deeply embedded in this new reality of constant resource scarcity.

As an academic library outsider, I'm not sure how the academic library is dealing with the resource constraints and fluctuations that are the new normal in higher education. My sense is that the academic library has historically been better at protecting your most important asset, your people, than other areas of academe. Dollars for journals, collections, and databases may be scarce (and getting scarcer), but my sense is that given the choice to protect a library job or to drop a particular subscription in time of fiscal decline, most libraries will choose to protect their people. This strategy, however, has its limits.

Core information services can be cut back only so far before the fundamental educational and research missions of higher education begin to materially suffer. The academic library, like every other part of the academic organization, will need to find new economic strategies for sustainability. Incremental cuts in costs and improvements in services will no longer be enough. Successful academic leaders will increasingly need to collaborate and partner with those traditionally tasked to develop new resources. Fundraising and grant writing will no longer be the sole purview of top leadership or development officers. An ability to identify and pursue new resources will increasingly serve to differentiate emerging academic leaders for promotion within and across academic institutions.

In thinking about big changes that your college and mine will experience in the years to come, there are a number of forces that will form the backdrop for our ascent into leadership positions. Of these forces, I see three as major themes that will define our work: competition, technology-induced change, and learning as a competitive differentiator. Let's take each in turn.

Competition

Higher education is a competitive business. One metaphor that seems to have captured the imagination of many postsecondary leaders is the Red Queen hypothesis. This hypothesis is drawn from Lewis Carroll's 1871 book *Through the Looking Glass*, where the Red Queen says to Alice, *"Now, here, you see, it takes all the running you can do, to keep in the same place."*

In higher education, we are all running as fast as we can just to keep up with everyone else. What do we compete for in higher education? A partial list would include rankings, status, students, faculty, public dollars, grant funding, philanthropy, brand awareness, and attention. The dimensions on which our institutions compete are interrelated and highly correlated. The number and quality of students applying to each institution closely follow our rankings. Our rankings determine our status. Our status drives, and is driven by, our success in generating giving (philanthropy). Some schools compete for the best basketball or football program, with the belief that competitive success on the court or the field will drive awareness, alumni giving, and student applications. Similarly, schools have competed to have the best departments and the best scholars, as comparative excellence in research is thought to translate into other advantages such as greater status and funding.

Much of my day-to-day work involves understanding how the state-of-the-art advances in teaching and learning, and then trying to organize structures and resources so that my institution does not get left behind. The arguments that I make for scarce resources are about carving out (and building upon) areas of strength and differentiation. The competitive domain that I am working in encompasses student learning. Digital learning initiatives are only a means to an end, with the ultimate goal being the improvements in student academic success.

I wonder what a comparative role would be in the academic library world? Who in your academic library is tasked with having a really good understanding of innovations at your peer institutions? Who is paying close attention to the non-incremental advances in academic library services? My hypothesis is that the need to understand the academic library competitive environment has never been greater. Networking within a range of communities will be a necessary pathway to library leadership positions for an aspiring academic librarian. The road to academic library leadership will involve both doing good work in your local environment and building a demonstrated track record of contributions and connections to the larger academic library and postsecondary communities.

The specific advice I have is to think about your work using a larger competitive framework. Become an expert not only in the work that you are doing at your school but how that work looks at your peer institutions. The beautiful thing about academics is that we are able to simultaneously compete and share. We are open about our operations, best practices, and struggles because we are all working toward the same mission. Competing with your peer institutions can go hand-in-hand with helping your peer institution. In fact, you want to develop a reputation as someone who is working for the larger benefit of your profession. I have found that some of my closest colleagues are people who work at schools that desperately compete with my own for attention, rankings, and resources. Being active in professional associations, really contributing and giving back, is not an option for anyone looking to ascend to a leadership role. It is essential that you leverage the resources, networks, and information that can be gained through an active professional life outside your institution to improve the practices inside your institution.

Technology-Induced Change

Technology is enabling new competitors to incumbent institutions to emerge from both within and outside our industry. This competition is coming from entities that offer products that seem similar to what we provide—courses, degrees, diplomas, and credentials. The competitive landscape now moves at the speed of technological change. All of our institutions are under enormous pressure to evolve rapidly to maintain whatever differentiating strengths we enjoy. In my world of teaching and learning, the need to transition from traditional residential lecture-based delivery modes to blended learning, flipped classrooms, and low-residency/online courses is acute. Figuring out how to incentivize and train faculty, fund the construction of classrooms designed for active rather than passive learning, and set up new online programs is never ending. We pay careful attention to what our colleagues are doing in learning innovation at our peer institutions. Developing a network of peers at other campuses to best understand the state of the art in teaching and learning is absolutely critical to having any chance of success at the campuses where we work.

My sense is that the academic library world is at the forefront of technologically driven change. Library spaces are transforming from repositories of content (books, journals) to vibrant collaboration and service spaces. The academic librarian, as navigator of the abundant data now available at the swipe of a phone, is more important than ever to adding value to the commodity that information has become. No longer is the number of books in the collection a differentiator for academic libraries. Rather, academic libraries that seek to contribute to their institution' ability to stand out in a competitive higher education market must do so in nontraditional ways.

Looking at technological change through a competitive institutional lens may be a challenge to us academics. The idea that we are part of an institution that is competing in a marketplace for scarce goods (be that good students, prestige, or dollars) may not be how we think about our jobs. The idea that a leadership role at our institution means doing everything possible to differentiate our institution in this crowded competitive landscape, to win this competition, may also feel off-putting. My argument here is that leaders and emerging leaders in higher education, including academic libraries, need to think about technology as a strategic force for competitive differentiation. We need to be able to leverage technology to lead change. This change is not undertaken for change alone but rather with the larger goal of improving our institutions' economic viability and sustainability. If you are not connecting the bottom line of the financial health of your institution to the work that you are doing as a campus leader then you will not be a campus leader for long.

The key when thinking about change, competition, and technology is to understand technology as a means rather than an end. How can you leverage technology to reach your larger organizational, service, department, or unit goals? How can you use technology to improve the services that your department offers? How can technology be leveraged to shift resources away from commodity or low-value operations and toward high-value operations? In the academic library world, I think this means finding as many resources as possible to pay for as many academic librarians as possible. Academic librarians, along with their fellow library staff members, are the people who build strong relationships with students and faculty. These sorts of relationships can't be scaled, and can't be replaced by new technologies.

My advice to you as you look to navigate your academic leadership career is to grasp just how important the understanding and proper use of technology has become. Technology is no longer the domain of the "technology professional." An understanding and ability to leverage technology cannot be constrained by the Library IT Director or someone with "digital" in their title. Whichever job you are in will require the strategic use of technology. Certainly, any leadership position that you aspire to will have a strategic technological component. Becoming comfortable with the language of technology, and the values and networks in the technology world, will be an essential tool in your leadership tool kit.

Learning as a Competitive Differentiator

We are truly in the midst of a learning revolution. Long-held assumptions of what instruction looks like are being challenged from all sides. The traditional lecture model has fewer and fewer defenders. Scarcities based on the number of learners that one educator can reach are being demolished by the development of free online courses. The system of credentialing, one based on seat time and the credit hour, is now being challenged by the competency-based education (CBE) movement. The question that I have for every leader and emerging leader in the academic library is—*how will you lead change in learning?*

The forces pushing for improvements in learning are coming from all sides. The proliferation of online learning programs has brought a new class of higher education employee, the instructional designer, to most campuses. These nonfaculty educators worked initially on online courses, often in online master's degree professionals programs aimed at an older student demographic. The instructional design techniques utilized in these online courses, however, translated well to residential courses. Every course benefits from well-thought-out learning objectives, and a course that is designed backward around the learning goals is preferable to the traditional desire to design it to "cover" the course content. The ubiquity of digital platforms, such as learning management systems (LMS), has also catalyzed the shift toward more blended teaching approaches for courses that have historically been completely lecture based.

The move to blended, flipped, and active courses is best accomplished when faculty partner with colleagues in other learning disciplines. Instructional designers, media educators, and assessment experts are increasingly working with faculty on course design. An academic librarian should also be a member of this course redesign team. How the academic library responds to this shift toward a team approach to teaching will, I think, largely determine the status and role of the academic library in the years to come.

At my institution, librarians are part of the teams that helped design our first low-residency master's degree program. Librarians are also key members of the teams working on our edX—open online learning courses. We also have a large-scale program to redesign our larger-enrollment introductory courses called the Gateway Initiative. Librarians are also members of the design team for the Gateway courses. Within all these creative course design teams, the academic librarians at my institution bring a set of specialized knowledge, skills, and resources that are essential for the course development. Library leadership has played an essential role both in articulating the value of librarians working on course redesign teams and in freeing up time and space for the librarians to engage in this collaborative work.

If the academic library is to play a leadership role in creating new models of teaching and learning, then I think the culture of the academic library may need to evolve along the same lines as the educational technology profession. All of us need to recast our roles as true partners and collaborators with faculty. Any verbiage that places us in a "support role" must cease. My insistence on partnership is not based on a narrow objective of preserving the privileges and positions of those of us currently occupying both academic library and educational technology roles. Rather, my argument for the academic librarian and educational technologist as faculty partner is based on the observation that creating these partnerships is the best method to assure high-quality student learning.

Tomorrow's academic library leaders will need to drive this change toward placing a librarian on the core teaching and learning team. Academic library leaders will need to articulate the argument as why librarians are essential in how colleges and universities will construct learning in the digital age. Librarians will need to create a seat at the table in the planning, development, and execution of new blended and online programs. Part of this shift of librarians away from support roles, and toward a collegial and partner role, will require a shift in how the academic library is organized. Working on teams to redesign and teach courses is incredibly time intensive.

Academic library leaders will need to come to grips with not only what new things can be done but also what things can be stopped. I don't know enough about the academic library to understand what services librarians can stop doing, but I do know that something will need to give. It is unlikely that a school will be hiring large numbers of new academic librarians. Leaders will need to drive a shift in priorities, job titles, and daily responsibilities in the academic library.

Bringing It All Together

In this chapter I've tried to argue that competitive and economic forces require our schools to make significant changes, and that a focus on learning will be critical for the long-term success of the institutions where we work. Further, I've tried to argue that the academic library, and the academic librarian, is well positioned to take a leadership role in driving these necessary institutional changes. The call to you is to look beyond the narrow organization of your own academic library and to think about your work in the context of the entire institution. This wide lens to your work as an academic librarian is no longer reserved to the people at the top of the organizational chart. Rather, it is your responsibility to lead change from where you are in the organization—and a commitment to leading change will be the defining attribute of anyone wishing to move up in the academic library world.

As a non-librarian, someone who has an office in the main campus library but is not part of an academic library organization, I am actively looking for library partners interested in working with me to drive institutional change. I seek to identify, collaborate with, learn from, and try to bring resources and attention to those librarians who are catalyzing non-incremental change at my institution.

The claim that the academic library is central to any efforts to advance learning at our colleges and universities is probably not a controversial one among academic librarians. The friendly push that I'm giving is for the academic librarian to more forcefully and more widely articulate this claim.

Getting involved in learning innovation projects and participating as colleagues in the teams that are spinning up new online and blended programs is an essential element in advancing this narrative. Placing the work of the library to advance learning as part of the larger strategic efforts of the institution is another effort that should receive your time and focus.

As an emerging and aspiring leader in your academic library organization, you need to make your contribution to non-incremental change visible. This means developing a strong understanding of the competitive forces at work within the academic library world, within your institution, and across higher education. Your career success will be governed by the extent to which you can be bilingual in talking about both library and institutional priorities, and can connect the two for colleagues both within and outside the library. Your greatest career risk is to swap management for vision, steady state improvements for fundamental alterations in structures and services. The protective bubble that wrapped around much of higher education in the years of enrollment growth and robust federal funding has come to an end. Higher education must change, learning must improve, and the academic library is well placed to be part of leading that change.

REFLECTIONS: KEY LESSONS FOR LEADERS

» Scarcity is the new normal in higher education, including the academic library

» Effective leadership will require new ways of thinking and doing things, not just competent management and incremental improvements to existing operations

» Forces of competition, technology, and new models of learning create both enormous challenges and opportunities for tomorrow's academic leaders

References

History of the Dartmouth College Library. http://www.dartmouth.edu/~library /home/about/libhistory.html?mswitch-redir=classic (Accessed May 2015).

"The Red Queen Hypohtesis." Wikipedia. https://en.wikipedia.org/wiki/Red _Queen_hypothesis (Accessed May 2015).

—— 4 ——

STUDYING LEADERSHIP DEVELOPMENT:
A JOURNEY FROM FRONT LINE TO DEAN'S OFFICE

Irene M.H. Herold

///////////// TOP TAKEAWAYS IN THIS CHAPTER

» There are multiple paths on your road to leadership; you can learn leadership from all of them

» Take advantage of the unconventional opportunity

» Work and educational experience shapes leaders

» Studying leadership development may leave you with more questions than answers

» Leadership is learned on the job and in professional development programs; good leaders bring the lessons together

There are many pathways along the leadership journey. The reasons a person takes one route versus another may be unclear. As one travels, one may not always have a clear sense from the start how the choices along the way contribute to create a whole route to a destination. My story exemplifies this. While I knew I aspired to a leadership position, how to get there was a mix of drive, ambition, and good fortune. How I view leadership changed through my scholarship during and after earning my Ph.D.

This chapter examines three pathways along my route to my current thinking about leadership: career, association work, and education. I then explore why I decided to study leadership development and the new discoveries and insights that emerged from what I learned. I'll conclude with a few thoughts about what leadership is.

Career Pathway

When I was a public school teacher, I discovered I relished being in charge of my classroom. I could be creative in curriculum design and enjoyed the learning process and seeing students engage with the materials. After a while I started to think about an administrative role but I had no interest in taking on the disciplinary responsibilities of a vice principal on the way to the top position of principal. When I was in elementary and junior high school I volunteered in the library. Not only did my family use the traveling bookmobile but we also made weekly trips to the public library. As an educator, I collaborated intensely with the school librarian where I taught, bringing in my classes for bibliographic instruction, research, and pleasure reading. Considering new paths for my career, I decided to enter library school as a conscious choice of aspiring to an administrative position. I took every course offered on library management and administration, in addition to the core curriculum. I found a passion for academic librarianship and have never regretted leaving public school teaching. Everything I learned as a schoolteacher contributed to my abilities and informed my actions as I traveled the path to library leader.

My first aspiration was to a library director's position, which I secured after working at a small private liberal arts college for six years as a frontline librarian. During this time I managed large projects, learned and worked in almost every department, held leadership positions in state library organizations, and served as interim director for three months. It was my enthusiasm and willingness to learn all areas of library services that prepared me for the director's role in a small college environment. I knew a little about everything and some areas in depth. I knew enough to understand my employees' work and in a pinch to help out, which is what a small-shop environment encourages. I loved feeling useful and coming up with solutions to move the library forward.

I viewed the experience as "being in charge." Because this was my first director position, one of the board of trustees members, who had connections with a private small Ivy League college, provided me with contacts from another area library director, whom I visited and who visited me. I also participated in the College Library Directors Mentor Program (CLDMP). The

CLDMP was open only to college library directors in their first year at institutions with a student full-time equivalency of 3,500 or less. It included a mentor, exchange of site visits, a closed listserv of current and past participants and mentors, and a three-day face-to-face seminar before the American Library Association's Midwinter Conference.

One of my strengths as a librarian was my instruction background. There was no formal library instruction program at my new institution. I set about helping them develop a set of learning goals based on a spiraled taxonomy and encouraged the public services librarian to apply for the Association of College and Research Libraries (ACRL) Immersion Teacher Training Program. When this librarian returned from the immersion experience she said, "I now understand what you're talking about and expect. I knew when you were hired there would be change but I didn't think I would have to change." She then thanked me for the experience and resigned. By giving continuing education to the public services librarian so she could meet my expectations, she learned that while my vision was worthwhile, it was not something she wanted to be a part of. It was a crucible moment in my development as a leader. I began to understand that not everyone loves to do what I love to do, and that sometimes to keep an organization healthy, some folks need to be supported in moving on.

After my second year as a director, I was recruited to consider applying for a director's position at a public liberal arts college with a significantly larger student enrollment and budget and an employee group of library faculty and staff. I turned down the opportunity to apply the first time but after they conducted a failed search and recruited me again in my third year, I decided to apply. The budget situation at my first institution was a huge factor in my decision to move on. I was ready to be at a more financially stable place. As part of my negotiations for this position, I asked for participation in the ACRL/Harvard Leadership Institute for Academic Librarians. After 18 months on the new job, I attended the institute in the summer of 2003. There we read Lee G. Bolman and Terrence E. Deal's work *Reframing*

> **It was a crucible moment in my development as a leader. I began to understand that not everyone loves to do what I love to do, and that sometimes to keep an organization healthy, some folks need to be supported in moving on.**

Organizations: Artistry, Choice, and Leadership, which introduced the concept of viewing an issue through different lenses to ensure a leader is utilizing effective approaches to leadership situations. Within four years in this second director's position, my title was changed to dean of the library. This was in recognition of the role I played on the campus and expanding responsibilities.

The terminal degree for librarians is the Master of Library Science. Just as I recognized that I would need a second master's degree for career mobility, which I earned in history, I also understood that as a library dean I wasn't viewed as equal to the other campus deans, who were all Ph.D.s. While initially I denied there was a difference between my ability to perform at a dean's level and my fellow deans, I came to understand that if I wanted to embrace the dean's role in higher education, I needed the earned doctorate. I searched for programs to enhance my administrative and leadership abilities. I found a program that was perfect for me; it focused on managerial leadership in the information profession. The coursework not only reinforced my intuitive practice but also gave me the theoretical knowledge to back up chosen courses of action. I was no longer a library manager but now also a scholar leader. The bonding and campus caché from sharing "war stories" about the dissertation process gave me entrée to conversations and interactions with campus faculty and administrators that I now knew I had been missing. I also now brought more to the table when discussing analysis of issues and approaches to problem solving.

Upon completion of my Ph.D. and with the imminent graduation of my child from high school, I started thinking about new positions. The president and provost had moved on and it felt like the right time for me to move on too. There were very few geographic locations that my partner would consider and I wasn't interested in changing jobs for a lateral career move. I wanted new challenges and growth opportunities. After careful consideration I applied to two institutions and was in the very fortunate situation of having to decide which job to accept. I am now employed at a research-intensive Association of Research Libraries institution. I went from an employee group of 24 to 165 and from a budget of several million to one of $15 million.

Association Work Pathway

When I was still working as a schoolteacher, I gained my first exposure to association work. Initially, I was elected to serve as my education association political action chair and then as the vice president of the association. My father had been an elected official and was very active in our hometown community. My mother volunteered with a variety of organizations and arts groups. My parents were my model for what professionals did, and part of that was serving their community.

My education association experience was followed by my career as a librarian, where in my first position I created a congressional district group and was elected to serve the Illinois Library Association GODORT (Government Documents Round Table) Forum as secretary and then manager. I applied for and was awarded the Readex/GODORT/American Library Association (ALA) Catharine J. Reynolds Award, which allowed me to attend a national government documents conference. I was a campus representative to the Associated Colleges of the Midwest's Women's Concerns Committee.

In my first director's position, I served the New Hampshire College and University Council's Library Committee as chair and volunteered to serve on a regional ACRL program committee. The longer I was in the state, the more responsibilities I took on at the statewide level, creating a mentoring and job shadowing program, and I began my national service. With my second director and later dean's position, I began serving on committees with two ACRL sections, eventually serving as chair of one of the sections and on some ACRL-level committees. I was then recruited by the ACRL Leadership and Recruitment Committee to stand as a candidate for the position of ACRL Board Director-at-Large.

One reason I wanted to serve as a director-at-large was to determine what the work of the ACRL board was and figure out if I was interested in running for the vice president/president-elect position. Perhaps it was a bit arrogant and naïve of me to presume that anyone would want me to stand for election for the top position. At first I thought I wouldn't want the vice president/president-elect position, but as I came to understand better how ACRL runs and what individuals may contribute to the association, I began to see taking the leadership role as a way to give back to the organization. During my last year as a director-at-large I was nominated and then elected to stand for service as the 2015–2016 ACRL vice president/president-elect.

In addition to library association work, I was also active in the Keene branch of the American Association of University Women. Through this organization I was selected as the representative of New Hampshire to serve a three-year term to Vision 2020 to work on equity issues. I enjoyed using my voice to advocate on issues where I felt passion.

Education Pathway

In preparation for my career as a teacher, I earned my bachelor of arts degree in English with a concentration in Behavioral Science and a secondary teaching certification. I thought about entering library school then but allowed a secretary to scare me off when she asked me, "Why do you want to go to library school?" I was flustered by her question and thought, "Why do I want to go to library school?!" I had no response. I hadn't yet obtained a teaching position and was merely exploring career alternatives. I promptly turned around and fled her office.

Prior to the requirement that teachers in Washington State earn a master's degree, earning a fifth-year certificate during a new teacher's first three years of employment was required. It was considered continuing education. One of the more enduringly valuable courses throughout my work life has been Educational Psychology. In addition to the methods and other required courses, I studied history and enrolled in the Puget Sound Writing Program (PSWP). The PSWP not only taught how to teach writing through experiential writing but also required the delivery of a one-credit, in-service course in one's home district. Teaching other teachers was an opportunity that led to the perception by those in the course that I was an expert. I was then invited to create district curriculum incorporating the use of computers into the writing process— something that sounds quaint today but was cutting edge back then.

After a decade, I decided it was time to change careers and enrolled in library school. I had taught nine years, mainly at the middle-school level with one foray into high school. I had taken a year off to follow my partner to Germany, where I taught English to adults, high school, and middle school students. A friend was just finishing library school and had secured a job at the Library of Congress as a Russian materials cataloger. I asked her if I would have to shelve books or if I could learn management in library school. She assured me that librarians generally don't have to shelve books. That was enough for me to enroll—ignoring that secretary's harsh question.

After working three years as a frontline librarian, I realized that if I wanted options for mobility within the profession, I needed to earn a second master's degree. A nearby university offered possibilities, and while contemplating which program to choose, I attended a Minor League baseball game. I just happened to sit with a sociology professor from my college, whose partner was chair of the history department at the university in a neighboring city. I asked him about the education department, the anthropology department, and finally mentioned that I had taught U.S. history for seven years, stating that maybe I should try applying to the history department. He was incredibly enthusiastic and encouraged me to apply. A few weeks later I received a letter telling me that I had been accepted into the history department's master's degree program, asking me to to fill out the application form and send my Graduate Record Examination (GRE) scores and transcripts!

Although my entrance into the program was unconventional, the experience with that department was wonderful. I enjoyed every course and opted to do the thesis versus a comprehensive examination to earn the degree. In the middle of all of this I had a child, which slowed my progress, as did changing jobs and moving to a different state. It took me seven years to complete that degree, learning so much about research and enjoying the process. I then started to look at Ph.D. programs but wasn't sure whether it should be in history or library science.

A colleague told me about the Managerial Leadership in the Information Professions Ph.D. program. It was offered at Simmons College in Boston and was supported through an Institute of Museum and Library Services (IMLS) grant, so the first few cohorts were tuition free. The first cohort had already started so I applied for the second cohort. I drove two hours for the entrance interview and on the drive home was convinced I wouldn't be offered a spot. I was wrong. There were 36 applicants for six student spots. Just as attending a baseball game changed my life, this was a career turning point. Earning my doctorate led me to think differently about leadership.

Key Moments and Questions

In thinking back over this journey, the mixture of fortuitous events and hard work leap out. What would my career have been if my younger self hadn't been flustered by a gruff secretary? I believe my library career was enriched from my teaching experience, which I wouldn't have had if I had attended library school directly upon completion of my undergraduate degree.

If I hadn't attended that baseball game, would I have developed a passion for research and decided to pursue a Ph.D.? If I hadn't earned the Ph.D., would I have been viable and able to have mobility in my career? What if I hadn't volunteered to serve or agreed to stand for election at different points along my journey? Would I still be perceived as a leader without these experiences? Am I considered a leader because of these experiences?

Why Study Leadership?

Participating in the two leadership development institutes previously mentioned, CLDMP and the ACRL Harvard Leadership Institute for Academic Librarians, exposed me to selected leadership studies, theories, and approaches, and also gave me a network of colleagues interested in developing their leadership. I also attended the Women's Leadership Institute, which was open to professionals from fields other than academic librarianship. Knowing that others were asking similar, and sometimes the same, questions helped reinforce my leadership vision and approach.

When I decided to apply to the Ph.D. program, then offered by Simmons College on Managerial Leadership in the Information Professions, I perceived it as something directly applicable to my position as an academic library dean. I viewed it as applied theory and practice. Because I already held the leadership position for the library on my campus, I had practical and not just theoretical experiences related to the readings on which to draw, while the others in the cohort were engaged in creating fictional scenarios. Many of them had leadership experiences as assistant and/or associate director or deans, but there was a difference. Lacking experience as a library dean, when the scenario coursework required a response as the top library leader, they could only speculate on the answer. I was also in a position to take what

What sustained me to complete the Ph.D. was my passion to understand leadership development.

we learned and immediately apply it on the job, which was a luxury the others didn't have. For example, during the class on fund-raising, the case statement I developed for an assignment was something I actually used to raise $50,000 during that semester.

While in my case the program was at times applied, as I was the only one in my cohort who held a dean's position, it was so much more. I learned about theoretical frameworks, how to set up and execute a research study, and how to critically examine someone else's study. I no longer read research articles in the same way and now know which questions to ask about validity and reliability, same size, and methodologies. I think about leadership differently too. Through exposure to a large number of theories and applying analysis to a leadership development program, my dissertation research and writing shifted how I interpret and accept results and evidence.

One of my thoughts on entering the Ph.D. program was that I would learn how to do social science research. I did. I also learned that while I truly enjoyed the end result, I didn't enjoy doing quantitative research. Quantitative research is more about collecting data and measures, using statistical analysis, and discussing how far from a null hypothesis a result occurs. I am a historian at heart and qualitative research is the kind of research and writing I love—narrative inquiry, textual analysis, and grounded theory. Knowing this, what sustained me to complete the Ph.D. was my passion to understand leadership development.

Undertaking a three-year Ph.D. program with a deep dive into leadership theory was totally different than attending a week-long leadership development institute. The CLDMP, a year-long mentorship program with a three-day face-to-face seminar, didn't even begin to scratch the surface of what it means to study leadership. It's true that some of the leadership theories introduced during the various institutes were highlighted during the Ph.D.

program, but in the Ph.D. program, they were put into the context of multiple other theories and explored for how they were developed, applied, and determined.

Doing this intensive study of leadership allowed the practice of applying different lenses through a variety of tools to leadership situations. From the first term there were assignments to write case studies, scenarios, and create a research proposal. A course in metrics and statistics for social science research was included with one in research methodologies. Topics of political information, government information, entrepreneurship, finance, and human resources rounded out the curriculum, highlighting ways to consider leadership beyond the daily operations of a positional job and within the greater higher education context. With this grounding, I could participate in a more knowledgeable way on my campus and within my state university system. I also contributed to revisions of accreditation standards regionally and felt secure in volunteering for a role on a national committee on scholarly communication and the research environment.

What I Learned About Leadership Development

Through my studies I learned that leadership, or rather leadership development, is not what I thought it was. Or rather, it is not what the majority of folks write about and describe as leadership. What we commonly accept as research about leadership development is usually about something else. Conventional thinking about leadership development typically takes the stance that exposure to a series of concepts, practices, and commonly displayed skills equates to the development program participant developing leadership expertise. My research concludes that while this construct of leadership being developed is anecdotally generally accepted, it doesn't appear to have been proven through causality-based research studies.

For example, some use a metric of career movement as a measure of leadership development when examining the effect a leadership development program has had on a participant. While the research may indicate that program participants move to new leadership levels a number of years later, this doesn't establish a causal relationship between program attendance and leadership advancement. Numerous other factors may cause change and advancement into leadership positions, including the personal motivations of an individual who enters a leadership development institute, unanticipated vacancies that require an individual to "fill in" a leadership position that was not sought, or "good old boys" networking where promotion is based upon who and not what you know. The participant may already have been on an upwardly administrative career path and participation in the program may have had little or no impact.

A study that compares a randomly selected group who had the same number of years in the profession as those who attended an institute can show that people who participate in an institute are more or less likely than the control group to have changed jobs. It still fails to demonstrate that the participants developed leadership as a result of being in a leadership development institute. It doesn't disprove the causation but it doesn't prove it either. It can't be conclusively proven that career mobility after participation in a leadership development program equates with more leadership being demonstrated by the program participant development. It may just mean that an individual changed jobs. Furthermore, one can hold a positional leadership title but demonstrate little to no actual leadership. Leadership failures are hard to blame on leadership development programs. Nor have any researchers examined how much the expected outcome of attending a leadership program contributes to changes in behavior of participants after the program.

Knowing that exposure to leadership development via an institute may not have any concrete leadership development results, why do so many continue to participate in these institutes? According to my research on participation in leadership development programs, one benefit is having a cohort with whom to bounce ideas around about approaches to issues, while others felt they came away with new tactics to consider. Some feel validated after attending a leadership development program, since what they heard reinforced their own thinking. Many discussed the renewal they felt by being able to step away from their jobs for a few days and having the opportunity to read and reflect on big picture ideas and theoretical concepts beyond the daily determination of which tasks need to get done next. Often these are self-reported

> **Studying leadership and leadership development has made me a better leader. My studies have yielded no definitive definition of leadership. Instead, I now engage in thinking about leadership in a variety of ways.**

perceptions provided by evaluations completed at the end of a program or shortly after the end of a program.

What kind of study could be undertaken to demonstrate there was causation between institution participation and leadership development in an individual participant? Are there ways of studying leadership development and testing for validity and reliability other than self-reports, career movement, and anecdotal feelings? What kind of documentation would show change, whether enduring or not, as a result of participating in a program?

What I learned about leadership development is that it needs far more study and analysis. The many leadership theories, such as transformational leadership, emotional intelligence, and servant leadership, to name a few, describe what perceived-as-successful leaders do, but knowing a theory and developing leadership in an individual are not the same thing.

What Is Leadership?

Sometimes it is easier to say what leadership isn't. It is not managerial skills. It is not being an administrator. Although both management and administrative positions are often discussed as leadership positions—and they may be—they have to be about more than just managing and administrating to demonstrate leadership. Leadership is not just a set of skills, although many have studied people in positions of leadership and have identified similar skills, traits, and characteristics.

John Kotter staked out the difference between managing and leading in his work *Leading Change*. In it he describes a leader as an individual who creates a vision, aligns resources, generates buy-in to that vision, and implements it to achieve change. A manager makes sure policies and procedures are followed to produce stable, predictable results. Kotter also argues that the most successful leaders both manage and lead but lean toward more leadership than management. In another Kotter work, *The Leadership Factor*, he argues that leaders are made and not born, suggesting it is the combination of education, experience, and behavior that shapes leaders, and that it can be learned.

The phrase *emotional intelligence*, the ability to be aware of one's own and others' emotions and inspiring others to accomplish more than they thought they could achieve by guiding them through this awareness, was coined by Daniel Goleman. It moves away from defining leadership as a dichotomy between management and leadership. Being inspirational may seem more nebulous than the tasks of managing or creating a vision, but it's the end result that defines whether leadership happened with a focus on people.

Studying leadership and leadership development has made me a better leader. My studies have yielded no definitive definition of leadership. Instead, I now engage in thinking about leadership in a variety of ways. I think broadly about actions of others and their approaches. I look beyond leadership in librarianship and consider higher education leadership and my place in the academy. In addition to networks, I have studies and toolkits to refer to when considering the most effective way to accomplish shared goals and visions. I better understand a broader context for the work I engage in on my campus, nationally through library associations, and internationally through consortia and memberships in groups. Every experience I had along the way, from schoolteacher to union representative to frontline librarian to library leader to Ph.D. to ACRL vice president/president-elect, provided me with additional knowledge and strengths. The journey has shaped me, and I still don't know the final destination but I'm looking forward to what's next along the path.

REFLECTIONS: KEY LESSONS FOR LEADERS

» All experiences and opportunities have value

» The value of a program may be different than the stated outcome, but it will still have value

» Leadership development is a rich area needing more research

» Think about what you want to get from a leadership development program and then select a program most likely to meet that expectation

» Individuals have multiple pathways to leadership; know what yours are and what progress you are making toward your leadership goals

—— 5 ——

THE ACCIDENTAL MENTOR

Patrick José Dawson

///////////// TOP TAKEAWAYS IN THIS CHAPTER

» Library leaders have a responsibility to help develop future leaders

» Mentoring relationships can develop in formal and informal ways

» Dedicated coworkers often make the best accidental mentors

» We all have the potential to become a mentor

I recently had the opportunity to speak with an individual from an executive placement firm that works with higher education, including the placement of directors and deans in academic libraries. Two things from the conversation resonated with me. The first was how to identify individuals with the potential to become administrators and leaders in libraries, for which there is no magic bullet. The second was the lack of investment in succession planning on the part of current leaders. The second item, from the experiences of the individual with the firm, wasn't unique to libraries but rather is an issue shared equally across academia and business. The takeaway from the conversation is that individually we librarians, despite the existence of formal leadership and mentorship programs, have been remiss in our profession in both developing leaders and planning for the future of the profession.

Because established programs for mentoring exist, it's easy to believe that the issue is being addressed. However, there are many more individuals to mentor than exist programs to mentor them and not everyone with leadership capabilities can become involved in a formal mentoring program. From

We librarians, despite the existence of formal leadership and mentorship programs, have been remiss in our profession in both developing leaders and planning for the future of the profession.

an individual perspective, each professional librarian has the capacity and responsibility to the profession to work in developing the future leaders. There are actions that we can take to address this situation. They fit into a set of interpersonal dynamics I call accidental mentoring.

What, then, is leadership? Taken literally, the definition of leadership is the action of leading a group of people or an organization or the state or position of being a leader. But how does one become a leader? What makes an individual a leader and how does one lead? Those topics are the subject of other chapters in this collection. In this chapter, I'd like to discuss the importance of mentoring in helping develop leaders and as a means for succession planning. I will use my experiences as both a mentor and mentee to illustrate the importance of mentoring and I would hope this at least sparks an interest and investment in mentoring and succession planning with both current leaders and potential leaders in the library profession. I believe more emphasis needs to be directed into mentorship, because leadership potential is often nurtured and can be developed through mentorship.

Mentorship is not necessarily a crucible moment for leadership development. Not every mentor will experience a crucible moment with his or her mentee, but a situation can arise in which crucible-like experiences will help individuals know the self-discovery of leadership, and for that reason, it is very important. In my case, it wasn't a crucible moment but a moment of self-doubt that allowed a mentoring opportunity to take place. Years ago, an opportunity took me out of my comfort zone because it included new responsibilities and supervising peers. I was motivated to succeed in this new endeavor and assured my superiors that they made the right decision to place me in this role. When a more experienced colleague asked me if I was having difficulties, it made me realize how insecure I was in this new position. Simply by telling that individual that I hoped to become successful (probably stated in a more colorful manner), a mentoring relationship bloomed. The response I received was, "If people didn't think you could do this, do you think you would've been chosen?" This wasn't only a confidence boost but the crucible-like moment led to a rewarding mentoring relationship. This same colleague mentored me for a number of years. It still amazes me to think that it evolved from an "accidental mentor" situation that became much more.

Mentoring Takes Different Paths

Mentoring happens, be it planned, intended, or not. It can be deliberate, or, very often, accidental. There are indeed programs that encourage and promote mentorship, including those instituted and supported by the American Library Association (ALA), the Association of College and Research Libraries (ACRL), the Association of Research Libraries (ARL), and other national and state organizations. For a quick review of existing programs and mentoring trends in academic libraries, take a look at "A Scoping Review of Mentoring Programs for Academic Librarians." There are also programs within individual institutions to encourage and formalize mentorship. However, as observed by the individual from the placement firm, often so much time is spent simply doing one's job that a formalized structure of mentorship is not necessarily attainable or even considered. In some cases where mentoring is part of an assigned responsibility, it can feel more like a job responsibility or daily training task than an opportunity to develop a mentoring relationship and a means to help develop a mentee's career. In formal mentoring programs, the mentor and mentee sometimes feel that there's a script or formula that should be followed, and when they deviate from that path (from the perception of either the mentor or mentee or both), it can be an unrewarding and frustrating experience for those involved.

Mentorship is seldom included in job descriptions or evaluated in performance reviews, so there is usually no means for its inclusion or performance measure for its success. If formal mentorship is to be established, an understanding of the expectations and time commitment from each party and the desired outcomes can help avoid disappointment or frustration. The importance of mentoring, specifically to develop future library leaders, is emphasized in "Mentoring to Grow Library Leaders" and the subject of *Mentoring in the Library: Building for the Future*. However, unlike in the movie *Kung Fu*

Panda, there are no master mentors who will kick our butts in order to impart wisdom so we can fully reach our leadership potential. However, where the formal structure is lacking, the interactions and business of daily work is where accidental mentorship comes into play.

In many ways, most of the mentoring I received falls into the accidental category. Mentoring can, and often does, occur in informal situations. Individuals new to the profession are most often concerned with learning how to do their job rather than seeking out a mentor for advice on how to transition into a leadership role. As a new librarian, I was mainly concerned with the specifics of the tasks at hand and not focused on the future. I had my "work world," which occupied my thoughts and actions, and had no immediate concerns about the profession beyond my new job and responsibilities. (I have to note, this was pre-Internet and pre-"Just Google it.") AACR2 (Anglo-American Cataloguing Rules, Second Edition), the LCSH (Library of Congress Subject Headings), cutter tables, and the shelf list were my more immediate companions and concerns than seeking out a more experienced individual to talk to about trends in organizations, management, future developments in information delivery, and the vision of the library and how it integrated into the greater university vision and mission. The future was just too far away and I only wanted to learn my job and be a good cataloger.

I depended upon other, more experienced, staff members and librarians for advice and guidance on job functions and for interpretation and help with established policies and procedures. Still, mentoring was involved. Just as children are mentored and advised by parents and other adults and develop attitudes toward life based upon experiences and influences, training a new employee also can influence and mold attitudes and perceptions toward the work environment. Influences and interactions can lead to the development of attitudes and perceptions that in turn can then evolve into the "emotional intelligence" skills of self/awareness, self-regulation, motivation, empathy, and social skill enunciated by Daniel Goleman in his *Harvard Business Review* article "What Makes a Leader?" It would be erroneous to suggest that interactions between a

> **Where the formal structure is lacking, the interactions and business of daily work is where accidental mentorship comes into play.**

new hire and a seasoned employee will influence lifelong attitudes or heavily impact the development of the five aforementioned skills but these interactions will undeniably help a new employee experience positive reinforcement and encouragement. Training while in a new position does not in itself constitute mentoring, but during that training, mentoring can take place, and can take place accidently.

Role of the Mentor

I have been asked and have heard others ask, "What do I do as a mentor?" or "How do I mentor?" These questions can prevent individuals from becoming involved in a formal mentorship program. These questions are addressed in orientation sessions to formal mentorship programs and there are intellectual and human resources available to help those in the mentoring process. But what about informal mentoring? Informal mentoring involves sharing career experiences or choices you made that may apply to others on their path to leadership. Mentoring isn't necessarily the constant delivery of sage advice but rather offering suggestions and insight or helping achieve clarity from a different perspective. Giving someone ideas and options is often more effective than personal advice or prescriptive answers. Mentors also introduce their mentees to helpful colleagues or individuals with experiences or connections to share. It can be as simple as introducing a new librarian to one's personal professional network and encouraging that individual to become involved in the profession and build their own network to turn to for advice and opinions.

I want to distinguish here between a role model and a mentor. Role models change during our personal and professional lifetime, just as our attitudes and tastes change during our lives. Everyone at one time or another has someone that they look up to as an example to imitate. I remember trying to comb my hair to look like *Ziggy Stardust*, to dress like a Zoot Suiter, or to exude cool like Sonny and Tubs in *Miami Vice*. A role model is not necessarily a mentor. A role model represents the behavior or success that others would like to emulate; a mentor advises and imparts knowledge and experience that can be used in personal and professional development. Mentoring is a prolonged learning process and can come from a variety of sources rather than a single role model. This is where accidental mentoring comes in and why I believe we are mentored and we mentor throughout our lives and professional careers, whether we know it or not.

In my case, and perhaps because of the fastidious attention to detail involved in cataloging, I was blessed with individuals who trained and mentored me to pay attention to small details, look for the exceptions, consult with those who have in-depth experience, listen to input on issues, and try to find solutions within existing parameters. All of these touch upon the emotional intelligence skills laid out by Goleman and, more relevant to my situation, helped me begin to build a tool kit that I was able to utilize in moving into positions of management and leadership. All of this happened accidently. I did not actively seek this; it happened as part of work interactions that take place daily and it was not until later that I realized mentoring took place.

In their *Harvard Business Review* article "Discovering Your Authentic Leadership," authors Bill George, Peter Sims, Andrew McLean, and Diana Mayer argue there is no clear profile for the ideal leader. That's good to know because there is also no clear profile for the ideal mentor. We're all capable of mentoring. Mentoring in librarianship can come from peers, other librarians, other staff members, or from people outside libraries. Two positions that I held during my career allowed me to be mentored in an area outside what would be considered leadership and outside direct library work. Yet what I received from this mentoring had bearing upon my personal leadership development. And, this was accidental.

At one time I was Romance Languages Librarian and at another time Chicano Studies Librarian at two different institutions. As can be expected from the job titles, the major focus of the positions was collection development and reference work in specific subject areas. Although I had the educational and language fundamentals for the work, I knew I would need to learn more, so I reached out to others for help. I consulted the author of the bibliography *Literatura Chicana* to learn how titles were chosen for the bibliography and what made them essential to a subject collection. I consulted with teaching faculty and other researchers to learn about the literature, themes, issues, trends, and authors in these subject areas. Through these contacts I was able to meet and speak with many writers and critics and developed an expansive resource network to help me do my job. Because of the nature of the individuals I worked with, the interactions that took place were more than simply work related. I became part of a group that was more like a continual seminar on literature and life. In effect, I was doing what I should have done to develop skill sets for providing reference help and developing collections in these subject areas, but through these more casual than businesslike interactions with others, I was being mentored and it was usually accidental.

We're all capable of mentoring. Mentoring in librarianship can come from peers, other librarians, other staff members, or from people outside libraries.

I learned from and was mentored by a professor of and critic of Latin American literature and a critic of "Magical Realism." I can't define a crucible moment or experience that constituted this mentorship. I would describe it as a running commentary on life, work, and literature that contained pearls of wisdom I was able to call upon. I met and was mentored by active authors, critics, and playwrights in Chicano/Chicana literature and learned what life experiences had influenced their writings and beliefs, what their memorable crucible moments were, and how these moments influenced their writing and attitude about life and leadership. I also learned about their mentoring moments and about times when others helped them, advised them, and assisted in furthering their careers. I learned about publishing, small presses, nontraditional book vendors, and specialized bookstores. And I learned a lot about people and their motivations. It could be argued that I was just doing my job—I needed to do all of this to be a good resource for reference inquiries and to become a competent bibliographer. That fact is true and undeniable. However, it was through my interaction with these individuals and the experiences that they shared that accidental mentorship occurred. I learned things that have been relevant to my work as a manager and leader. I learned about passion for and love of your work and art and about focus and dedication from these writers and critics. I learned from the literary themes employed in magical realism that things are not always what they seem and that the perception and perceived reality of one person may be very different from that of another. This is a good mentoring lesson in itself. I learned that when you don't know, don't fake it; admit that you don't know and ask for help in understanding and learning. I learned that collectively, people are able to learn and to find solutions when working together.

Of course, it could be argued that this could have been developed in another way or gathered from other sources or individuals. Again, this is true; however, I believe that this mentoring by individuals that influenced me in areas that touched on management and leadership helped me develop the emotional intelligence that Goleman refers to. And more to the point of this essay, the mentoring I experienced was accidental and those who mentored me had no standard, clear profile of what a mentor should be.

Learning From a Leader

Although the accidental mentoring that developed during my career was viable and successful, if the opportunity arises, I would encourage those who are interested to become mentors or mentees through a formal mentorship program. There are mentorship programs and opportunities available through national and state library associations as well as through individual universities and colleges. I have been fortunate enough to be involved in formal mentoring programs during my career. As stated earlier, if mentoring is to be formal, parameters should be defined, expectations established, and assessments developed to ensure success. Thankfully, these have been vetted in established programs, but it is a good idea for the mentor and mentee to review parameters when initially engaging in a formal, structured program. Even with the large amount of literature available on mentorship, as is the case with leadership, there is no clear profile of an ideal mentor, so it's an opportunity for all to participate and learn during the process.

Mentorship can mean many things to individuals, and expectations can be varied. Early in my career, I was a library intern. In 1985 the University of California, Santa Barbara began a program for newly graduated librarians at Davidson Library to gain professional experience as a librarian and to help build a resume before seeking full-time employment in an academic library. Best of all, it was a paid internship, with all the benefits and responsibilities of a librarian in the University of California system. The original intent was to focus on librarians from under-represented groups to help diversify the ethnic and cultural composition of the academic librarian ranks. Unfortunately, because of legal limitations and court decisions, beginning with the *Regents of the University of California v. Bakke* decision and subsequent decisions by state and federal courts, the internship no longer is specifically tailored to under-represented groups but continues to exist.

The original purpose of the internship was of course to gain work experience in the basic functions of librarianship, being technical services, collection development, and public services, by working with experienced librarians who would assist and guide you. It was not explicitly stated, but the hope was that one of the individuals you worked with would also serve as a mentor to help in your transition from library school student to professional academic librarian. Also, the head of reference was appointed coordinator of the mentorship program and tried to align individuals to help the interns, but no formal mentoring relationship was defined. All of this represented noble endeavors, but planning was an issue.

Two of us were chosen to be the first interns in this new program—the program was the brainchild of the university librarian but it was a new program and a few issues became apparent. The first issue was that there was no agenda, which was good in that it allowed adaptation and flexibility. We were, after all, the first in this new program so it gave us room to improvise, adapt, and adjust as needed. From this experimental beginning, a more formalized structure was developed for subsequent interns. The second issue was that those who were to train and hopefully mentor us were unfamiliar with the expectations of the program, as the program was new and lacked defined parameters. Much refinement occurred in the first year, which resulted in a successful program. Finally, the issue was that there was no guidance for the individuals who were hoped to mentor us. Most had never been in a mentoring situation, so without formal training, it was hoped that experience would help guide us. I admit that the training and work-related advice I received was very good, but the mentoring aspect for career development was lacking at the time.

Functional training occurred for specific job duties, based upon the practices and policies at the Davidson Library, but mentorship for the profession as a whole or for leadership, management, or future thinking was initially lacking. To his credit, the university librarian who conceived and instituted the program stepped in to help. He began to meet with us weekly to discuss libraries, the library profession, trends that were developing at that time in academic libraries, and also management, leadership, and professional associations for librarians. He also related experiences and situations from his professional career that helped guide him to leadership. It is rare that the library director or dean takes the time to regularly meet with a brand new librarian, so this had a huge impact upon the two of us. The university librarian made time for us, gave very good advice, and made sure to introduce us to colleagues who could also guide us and help us become involved in ALA and other associations. His intervention helped define mentorship in the program and allowed for a satisfying experience for us—the first two interns. Dedication to diversity and helping individuals from under-represented groups grew within the profession, and this new internship program was destined for enduring success.

My takeaway from this experience was the importance of dedication. The first was dedication to a project. The university librarian was dedicated to seeing his internship program succeed and intervened as appropriate to provide the personal involvement and resources to ensure that it would. The second was a dedication to diversity. Unfortunately, the numbers of librarians from under-represented ethnic and cultural groups has not changed dramatically since 1984; however, the number of library administrators from under-represented groups has increased ever so slightly. The mentoring I received on the importance of diversity and inclusion has been invaluable to me and I have employed it in decisions I have made in the areas of management and leadership and hiring. And a good portion of it was through accidental mentorship.

From Accidental to Intentional Mentoring

I later became a mentor in the same internship program at the University of California, Santa Barbara. Based on my experiences in the program and from the mentoring I received in my career, I was happy to contribute to creating a structured program. Continuing in formal mentoring, I also participated as a mentor in a Spectrum Scholarship Mentorship program that was rewarding and had the benefit of defined parameters, expectations, and an evaluative process. Rather than go into the mechanics of the Spectrum Scholarship Mentorship program, I will note that it has been soundly developed by dedicated individuals who do the training for prospective mentors for the program. It is a rewarding and successful program and I encourage people to become involved in it and support it.

The mentoring I received on the importance of diversity and inclusion has been invaluable to me and I have employed it in decisions I have made in the areas of management and leadership and hiring.

From experiences during my career in libraries, starting as a cataloger to my current position as Dean of Libraries, many of the career choices and decisions I made were influenced by interactions with the individuals who have, in some way or another, intentionally or accidently mentored me. Purposeful mentorship occurred through the structured programs I have had the privilege and opportunity to be involved with and accidental mentorship developed from my work and personal interactions that evolved into mentoring. The latter was not always fully appreciated for its value in the moment but always later in retrospect. I have striven to continue this process by using interactions with newer librarians, or even those whom I speak to and recruit to consider becoming librarians, as an opportunity to do a bit of mentoring. Not in an overbearing manner, and avoiding being pedantic or condescending, I simply try to call upon what I have learned through my personal and professional experiences that may be of help to someone who is making career choices or choices involved in pursuing a role in leadership and management.

What, then, are the major takeaways from this narrative? The first is that mentoring works. Goleman writes, "It has repeatedly been shown that coaching and mentoring pay off not just in better performance but also in increased job satisfaction and decreased turnover. But what makes coaching and mentoring work best is the nature of the relationship." The relationship can be defined by the mentor and mentee: it can be a formal relationship, such as through an established mentorship program, or a relationship through an informal agreement between the two parties. It can also be accidental, which happens everywhere and all the time.

Second, there is no standard for what a mentor should be; there is no checklist nor personality profile for being a mentor. All that is needed is the desire to help, engrained in us as librarians, along with a desire to ensure that the future of the profession is in capable hands for the next generations. These are values that almost all librarians share, and translating these values into action through mentoring is not difficult. The time involved in the mentor–mentee relationship is not defined nor prescribed. In formal programs, it sometimes ends when the formal program ends, but sometimes the relationship endures.

The same is true in informal or accidental mentoring. It may end when a common bond is no longer there or when one of the two takes a new career path or develops a new group of associates. However, I can say from experience that these relationships can last for years. Also, mentoring is not a one-way street. The mentor can learn from the mentee, and often the mentee has had experiences and can offer observations that are rewarding and give the mentor clarity. An example would be a newer-to-the profession librarian sharing their knowledge of technology with a more seasoned colleague. I haven't found any parameter that states that the mentor need be chronologically older than the mentee. A good mentor–mentee relationship is a give-and-take and each learns from the other.

Finally, mentoring can be, and in my opinion most often is, accidental. With that in mind, I try to gauge my connection with newer librarians in the manner of accidental mentorship, based upon interactions that were memorable and useful to me over my career. This does not mean being bombastic or trying too hard to be wise and insightful. It means being helpful, giving advice to someone with less experience in the profession, or introducing that person to others who may facilitate the discovery of leadership potential. That is the value of mentorship and how it can assist in developing new managers and leaders and can be used for succession planning in the profession.

//////////// REFLECTIONS: KEY LESSONS FOR LEADERS

» Mentoring works and should be encouraged and acknowledged

» Whether it is formal or accidental, mentoring relationships benefit librarians and their organizations

» Take a personal interest in new librarians and interns; get to know them and help them discover and develop their potential as future leaders

» Remember that new librarians look for a model, someone who has reached their aspirational goals; with that in mind, each interaction with new librarians has the potential to be a mentoring opportunity

» Remember how you were helped in your career path and endeavor to do the same

References

George, Bill, Peter Sims, Andrew N. McLean, and Diana Mayer. "Discovering Your Authentic Leadership." *Harvard Business Review*, v.85/2 (February 2007).

Goleman, Daniel. "What Makes a Leader?" *Harvard Business Review*, v.76/6 (November–December 1998).

Lee, Marta K. *Mentoring in the Library: Building for the Future.* Chicago: American Library Association, 2011.

Lorenzetti, Diane L., and Susan E. Powelson. "A Scoping Review of Mentoring Programs for Academic Librarians." *Journal of Academic Librarianship*, v.41/2 (March 2015).

Regents of the University of California v. Bakke. 438 U.S. 265 (1978).

Sears, Suzanne. "Mentoring to Grow Library Leaders." Journal of Library Administration, v.54/2 (February 2015).

Trujillo, Roberto G., and Andrés Rodríguez. *Literatura Chicana: Creative and Critical Writings Through 1984.* Oakland, CA: Floricanto Press, 1985.

University of California, Santa Barbara Library. "Library Residency Program: Evolving Workforce Residency." http://www.library.ucsb.edu/library-human-resources/library-residency-program (Accessed September 2015).

6

THE PATH TO LIBRARY LEADERSHIP: THE IMPORTANCE OF A LEADERSHIP PLAN

Trevor A. Dawes

///////////// **TOP TAKEAWAYS IN THIS CHAPTER**

» Develop a personal mission statement and refer to it often

» Build relationships with mentors—formal and informal

» Know your limitations

» Continue to learn and grow

Preparing leaders for the library profession is by no means a new phenomenon. However, as one looks at the number of leadership training and development programs, institutes, workshops, and conferences, one might ask the question, "Where are all the people who participated in these programs?" Some choose to remain in the library profession. Others leave, voluntarily or involuntarily, because of lack of opportunities. Still others will not be employed in positions that are traditionally thought of as leadership positions, though I would argue that these people are still leaders in their own right.

Although I believe that some qualities of leaders may be innate, several leadership qualities can be taught or developed and can be nourished under the right circumstances. At the start of my college career, it was never my intention to become a library leader; in fact, it wasn't even my intention to become a librarian. My leadership journey, highlighted in this chapter, will address the actions I took to develop those skills, as well as the support I received from family, friends, mentors, and colleagues that made it possible for me to be where I am today—an associate university librarian at a mid-sized university and a past president of a national library association.

I've mentioned two positional titles that I hold to describe leadership in my own career, but is holding a title the sum total of leadership? Certainly not! Early (1900 to 1929) definitions of leadership focused on control and power, such as those of Joseph C. Rost in 1991. However, by the 1940s, definitions began to incorporate elements of dealing with people and about the relationships among leaders and those being led. As the study of leadership began to grow and evolve, so did the definition. By the 1960s, according to Rost, there was "increasing support for viewing leadership as behavior that influences people toward shared goals." Definitions that include this concept of influence exist today, and those definitions are the ones I choose to use when I think about leadership.

Introduction

What are leadership characteristics? There is no simple answer. Leadership experts will often suggest that the skills or traits needed may be situational and that an effective leader will have the ability to adjust his or her style to the particular situation. Specifically, for library leaders, Peter Hernon and colleagues believe there are several "competencies and responsibilities of top management teams." They describe these competencies in their work *The Next Library Leadership: Attributes of Academic and Public Library Directors*, which include the following:

>> **Having a vision for the future**: Establishing and maintaining a culture that encourages staff to develop their maximum potential
>> **Developing staff**: Valuing and respecting the ideas of others
>> **Managing personnel**: Dealing with personnel consistently and fairly
>> **Planning and budgeting**: Preparing a budget to implement the goals and objectives of an organization
>> **Managing operations**: Planning, conducting, and participating in meetings so that the collective resources of the group are used efficiently and effectively

>> **Possessing political and negotiation skills**: relating library needs and goals to those of funding officials and agencies
>> **Engaging with the community**: Understanding the flow, use, and value of information in society as a whole and how this relates to the role of libraries
>> **Fund-raising skills**: Developing and writing proposals for state, local, federal, and private funds

Interestingly, these authors discuss what might be considered "hard skills." I would add to this list of competencies the following:

>> Communicating effectively (including having excellent listening skills)
>> Acting ethically
>> Managing time efficiently
>> Demonstrating empathy

This list could become lengthy. As we about a leader whom we admire, some characteristics of that person come to mind that may appear in the list above or that could be added to that list. This list of traits is therefore not exhaustive, nor can any list be. The leadership qualities above represent only a sampling of those that Hernon and colleagues describe. They, because of the volume of traits they identified in their research, categorized the traits as follows:

>> Planning
>> Protective work environment
>> Problem solving
>> Staff growth
>> Leadership (advocacy)
>> Leadership (donor relations)
>> Leadership (image/role setting)
>> Leadership (direct/manage change)
>> Leadership (strategic directions)
>> Educational attainment
>> Experience/prior activities

>> Professional growth/involvement/accomplishment
>> Professional presence
>> Personal characteristics (internal makeup)
>> Personal characteristics (dealing with others)
>> Knowledge areas (professional issues)

The above list demonstrates that there is no shortage of characteristics that we might look for in leaders. It would be impudent to think that any leader would—or could—have all of these qualities. However, as many leadership theorists will suggest, leaders should have the ability to adjust their style according to the situation. Being able to adjust your style may present its own challenges, but as Bill George and Peter Sims note in their 2007 work *True North*, leaders must live an authentic life—one that integrates the major elements of both the personal and professional self. The first 30 years are the formative years for any leader and several components comprise this stage. During these formative years, there are many ways to develop leadership skills—in the community, on sports teams, in student government, in employment, or in extracurricular activities. I found it important to participate in many of these activities because of my level of interest in them (student government, employment, etc.) or because I believed they would bring some benefit to others (community service work).

Participating in these activities helped me to acquire some of the characteristics that Hernon describes. Working as editor of my high school student newspaper, being elected to student leadership positions, and volunteering both in school and in the community helped to hone some of the skills and traits I believe have helped me on my leadership journey. I understand now, in retrospect, the importance of these experiences in shaping my present positions, as I continue to use—and improve upon—what I learned. I would continue to enhance my abilities through additional development opportunities once I determined my path.

Foundations of Leadership

Leadership development programs abound. I've participated in my share of these programs and learned from each one. However, the foundations of my leadership abilities began well before my participation in any of these programs. Having a supportive network makes a difference in how you develop as a leader, and my network began with my family.

Since I was young, my parents and siblings told me that I had an entrepreneurial spirit. These were not the exact words, which were more like, "You're a businessman," but that was the language of the day. My business sense at the time showed when I would take on the chores that my siblings were supposed to do—if they paid me to do it. Payment at the time didn't have to be in cash, though it often was. Payment could have also been extra time for me to control the TV channel (though there weren't many options at the time) or other "perks" that children might find exciting or rewarding. My siblings were all too happy to oblige. And although our parents didn't necessarily celebrate these activities, neither did they castigate them. Through these activities I developed a strong work ethic and a sense of self-worth—both of which are important for leaders to have.

That I wasn't discouraged from these activities was not, on its own, sufficient support. My ability to turn those earnings into savings or to gain some "independence" was definitely supported—and ultimately caught the attention of my siblings. I had the resources—and the time—to do some of the things I wanted to do and they also wanted a similar level of independence. I did not consider this experience "leadership" at the time but in retrospect, my actions and behaviors had a direct influence on my siblings. Information Today publishes the Accidental Series of books, in which librarians discover new roles for themselves as the nature of the work required in their libraries shifts. In a similar manner, I would describe myself—in this instance—as an accidental leader.

Support in the leadership journey goes beyond family. The familiar saying, "it takes a village" is just as apt when considering leadership development as it is when raising a child or supporting a family. A part of this village includes mentors and I am honored to have had many mentors—both formal and informal—in my career. Mentors play an invaluable role in leadership development. They can promote growth, encourage learning, impart knowledge, and provide advice. In the best mentor relationships, both the mentor and protégé learn from each other.

It is unlikely that anyone will dispute the value of mentors, but finding the right mentor—one in which there is a mutual relationship built on trust—can often be a challenge, but not an insurmountable one. Many library associations have formal mentoring programs; mentoring relationships can develop organically among colleagues, and some libraries have formal mentoring programs, although the expected outcomes of these programs will often vary. Some of the employer-sponsored programs are intended to acclimate new employees to the organizational climate and culture; others are geared toward preparing employees for the tenure and/or promotion process. In finding a mentor, it is helpful to know the area(s) in which you would like to be mentored.

My first library mentors were informal. I was a work-study employee in the library while an undergraduate student, and although I had no idea I wanted to be a librarian at the time, several librarians with whom I worked encouraged me to think about a career in librarianship. It is uncommon, I suspect, for high school students—especially young black males—to think about going to college to become a librarian. That certainly was not on my agenda. One of the librarians, however, who still remains a mentor today, is an African American male librarian. He kept telling me that I would make a good librarian and that I'd be a library leader. This librarian would also help me become active in professional associations. This relationship was an informal one. I was, after all, a work-study student with no desire to become a librarian. Seeing in me the qualities of both a librarian and a leader, he sought to encourage those.

I didn't believe I was performing exceptionally well—of course I was doing my best, and I had been, in my time as a student, promoted to a student supervisor position, doing the work of some of the full-time staff. I had occasion to interact, almost daily, with my mentor. We had formal meetings that were work related but we also had many informal conversations about a wide range of topics. Through these conversations he discovered that I was not committed to a particular major and therefore kept suggesting library school as an option. I appreciated, but didn't heed, the advice—at least not immediately.

It would be almost 10 years after completing my undergraduate studies, during which time I continued to work in libraries, until I completed my

Master of Library Science degree and began working in my first "professional" library position. I then realized I had internalized the advice I had received. I worked in an environment that was supportive of professional and leadership development and had the opportunity to participate as an attendee in a leadership development program for early-career librarians. I was assigned a formal mentor for this program. This mentor is an international leader in the field who

As one looks at the number of leadership training and development programs, institutes, workshops, and conferences, one might ask the question, 'Where are all the people who participated in these programs?'

travels and speaks extensively and is incredibly knowledgeable about the profession. Primarily because of his schedule, we weren't able to meet regularly or have impromptu conversations in the hallway. We did have formal scheduled meetings and would get together at conferences or other events. Although the relationship I have, and still maintain, with this mentor is different from the one I have with the previously mentioned mentor, both have been effective in providing support, guidance, career advice, employment references, and insight into the profession.

Through the first mentor I learned more about the profession and what it means to be a librarian. I also gained information about how to develop a career plan. At the time, he was a subject librarian at the university. He went on to become a department head, left that university for another, and is now a library dean at a different institution. We maintained our relationship throughout his moves and he shared information about what to look for when searching for a job, how to know if the job/institution is a right "fit" for you, and other tips on career planning and advancement. From the second mentor, I learned more about leadership development. As this was a formal relationship, created as a part of a leadership development program, we had more structured conversations about the topic of leadership—what it means, how to be an effective leader—and spoke some about what it's like being a director of a large, often complex library organization.

These two mentors provided different, but both rewarding, experiences. These experiences represent only two types of mentoring relationships that I have built with colleagues over the years. Although different in nature, they serve as examples of how a mentor/protégé relationship can be sustained over several years, even if the parties are not in the same institution. One of the keys to success as a leader is to find mentors who will steer you in the right direction. On more than one occasion I have called upon a mentor to help walk me through a situation that I was dealing with at work. Appropriate support from human resources offices is no doubt helpful, but I have found it helpful to check in with my mentor when I have a particularly thorny personnel matter about which I need some advice. The external perspective can be invaluable. These mentoring relationships will not only help with leadership or career development, they can also lead to long-term friendships. One of the principal benefits for me was gaining the ability to develop a leadership plan.

Great leaders empower and support others on their leadership journey. Just as I found mentors and have benefited from their expertise and counsel, I believe it's also important to be a mentor to others.

Developing a Leadership Plan

Having a personal mission statement is an important planning tool irrespective of the role you intend to play in libraries. This plan will provide the context for all your actions and can also serve as a motivational tool. The statement describes your purpose and incorporates the values that you hold dear. In developing a statement, one must be realistic and set goals that are a stretch but also attainable. Once goals are defined, the process for attaining them must also be outlined. Developing a leadership plan is very much like creating a mission statement for a library or any other organization. In this plan you envision where you want to be and what steps you need to take in order to get there. Developing my mission statement was a journey of self-(re)discovery and learning. The following are a few concepts—or, perhaps, guidelines—that I keep in mind when creating my plan:

>> Set S.M.A.R.T. (specific, measurable, attainable, realistic, and timebound) goals
>> Create an action plan to pursue the goals
>> Be open to new opportunities/be flexible

» Take time to reflect on experiences
» Help others learn
» Focus on strengths and make a development plan
» Seek feedback from a variety of trusted sources
» Remember that this is a process

There are numerous tools available to help one create a personal mission statement. Library leadership programs (or other non-library-specific programs) may include a component on how to set and achieve personal goals. One tool that I have used, and have recommended, is the "Values, Visions, and Missions Work Sheet" in the *1995 Annual*. The worksheet uses a process of "clarifying values, writing a vision statement, and then developing a mission statement." This step-by-step comprehensive process begins with sharing some principles of personal strategic planning, followed by questions designed to elicit your personal vision. Sample questions include the following:

» List some core values that have been important to you throughout your life
» Describe the career you want and the professional person you aspire to become
» Describe your distinctive competency

The vision statement then describes the person you want to be in three to five years. Using a set of established criteria, you then draft a mission statement that is very specific and serves as a guide for making professional and personal decisions. The worksheet ends with developing the strategies that will be used in attaining the goals.

I was first introduced to this worksheet when I participated in a leadership development workshop in the early 2000s and have been using it ever since. One example of its use was when I decided, in 2005, that I wanted to become president of a national library association within five years. As a first-time attendee of this conference in 2005, I was so impressed with the quality of programming and that the organization itself could put on such a relevant conference that I wanted to lead that organization. There will be moments, such as this experience for me, that have such an impact on you, they will help shape your future. I had recently started a new job, part of an earlier plan, and therefore needed to refresh my goals.

After securing support from my then library director, I stood for election to the board of the association. Despite an unsuccessful bid for a seat on the board, I continued to remain active in the association by actively participating in committees, chairing groups, and attending conferences. I also shared with almost anyone who would listen that I wanted to be president of the association and why. I was both surprised and delighted when, in 2011, the chair of the nominating committee of the association called to ask if I wanted to stand for election as vice-president/president elect. I was successful. The invitation to be a candidate came a year after my time frame and my term as president two years later, but I'm confident that establishing and actively working toward the goal enabled me to make it happen.

Over the years I have found other resources that help develop leadership skills and abilities. Providing more than just information on how to develop a vision, *One Piece of Paper* by Mike Figliuolo asks a series of questions to help develop the leader. Figliuolo helps to understand leadership philosophy, how to lead yourself and others, and how to lead a balanced life.

Whether one uses the Pfeiffer worksheet, *One Piece of Paper*, or some other resource to develop a vision and mission, the objective is the same: to plan that future desired state and the steps needed to get there. It's important to review the plan regularly to ensure that you're on target (I keep mine posted on a bulletin board in my office where I can see it). Be sure that decisions you make are consistent with the plan, although it's also important to maintain a certain amount of flexibility. There may be circumstances that require a course correction—whether slight or major. The time frame may need to be adjusted or new goals set altogether if the goals are reached in advance of—or after—the stated time frame.

Invest in Yourself

Leadership development is never complete. Setting a vision and determining goals are a part of the development process, but so is continuous learning.

Like finding a mentor, learning may be formal or informal. Formal leadership development programs for librarians are described extensively in *Creating Leaders: An Examination of Academic and Research Library Leadership Institutes*. Irene M. H. Herold identifies and critiques several national leadership development programs, many of which are still extant. Some state, regional, and local library associations offer leadership development programs, as do individual libraries and library consortia. Informal learning also happens in a variety of ways—for example, through networking at conferences or online.

After developing a personal mission statement, aspiring leaders should consider participating in a leadership development program. The program of choice should be based on the desired outcomes and whether or not that program is designed to meet those needs. I knew fairly early, after I began working in libraries, that I wanted to lead in some capacity. My mentors also affirmed that I had leadership qualities. Before even beginning my library science program, I earned a master of arts degree in educational administration, understanding the benefit this would have for academic library positions. This program included courses on human resources management, budgeting, student services, and private school leadership. These courses would serve me well later as I assumed positions of greater responsibility in libraries.

I wanted, however, to get a better sense of library leadership programs and to find out if there was something else to be learned in a more controlled and focused setting. It was at this point, and after I received my library degree, that I participated in my first library leadership development program, aimed at early-career librarians. In addition to covering the basics of leadership theory, this program concentrated on library assessment techniques, understanding and developing leadership styles, and networking. Years later I would participate in two additional leadership programs where we concentrated on topics that included collaborating with information technology (IT) colleagues, understanding the higher education landscape, enhancing presentation skills, project management, and networking.

One of the primary benefits common across all programs, however, is the network of colleagues with whom I shared the experience. The tangible takeaways about leadership theory, project management, presentation skills,

If asked the question 'Are leaders born or made?' I would have to answer 'Both!'

and more are all invaluable. I cannot overstate the value, however, of having a group of colleagues on whom you can call with questions or when you want to get advice, or just to have a conversation with about a problem or issue. Many colleagues who have been through similar programs also share this sentiment. The lesson I learned from these programs is that as much learning happens in the classroom as happens outside the classroom and that it is important to maintain positive relationships with my cohort members, as they provide a strong support network.

It's generally expensive to participate in these programs. Obtaining financial support from your employer is the best way to achieve participation. Other development programs, however, such as those offered by state or local organizations, tend to be less expensive. Cost will often be a factor in determining whether to participate. The cost of the program should not be a deterrent because I've always believed that one should invest in oneself. With the rise of massive open online courses (MOOCs) and other affordable online learning options, there is practically no excuse (short of the time it takes to make the investment) to continue learning.

Failure Is an Option, or, Know Your Limits

It can be difficult to find time to develop the skills needed to be an effective leader. Creating that time and space to learn, however, is critical and is one of the most significant investments you can make in yourself. One way to continue learning and developing is through volunteer service. This service may be in professional associations, religious groups, or civic organizations— whichever organization engages in work that you're passionate about and one in which you'll be able to commit to the work.

Most of my volunteer activities have been with professional associations, at both the state and national levels. I've served on or chaired numerous committees, task forces, and work groups. However, volunteering is the easy part. Following through on your commitments may be less easy. Be sure to do what you say you're going to do. By acting on your words you gain the trust and respect of your colleagues and other leaders, and this may lead to leadership opportunities. Managing your reputation and demonstrating your leadership capabilities requires that you volunteer in moderation and do not overcommit your time. Remember that you still have a full- or part-time job at which you also need to perform well. It's also crucial to find the right work–life balance. It means developing the ability to say "no." It is satisfying to be recognized for your work and to be invited to participate in new or different activities, even those about which you are passionate, but understanding the level of commitment the assignment will require, in addition to your other obligations, will help make a decision on whether or not to accept the offer. Most people will understand when you turn down an opportunity if you're honest about why you're unable to do it.

Leaders understand the value of taking risks and can often determine the level of risk involved in an action before pursuing that course. Taking risks, whether personal or professional, can teach you about yourself and what you need to succeed. Some people are afraid of taking risks for fear of failure or because the risk may move us outside our comfort zone. But taking risks—calculated risks—can be fulfilling. When evaluating risks, there are several factors one might consider. These factors include the following:

>> Is this risk consistent with my values?
>> What other choices do I have?
>> What will happen if I don't pursue this course of action?
>> What is the motivation for taking this risk?
>> What might the expected results of this action be?
   What will change?
>> What will be the effect of this action on others?

There may be other factors to consider based on the specific action to be taken, but you may ask these questions before acting on anything that is a perceived risk.

Taking a risk means you're willing to try something new in order to succeed. It also means you are willing to be unsuccessful (to fail?) Failure without reflection is not an option. Even if the action doesn't yield the results you expected, you should analyze the situation to glean any lessons that may prove helpful for the next action. I made reference earlier to my unsuccessful attempt to be elected to the board of a national library association. Although I was disappointed by the election results, I came to realize that I wasn't ready for that role at the time. My mentors and other colleagues continued to provide support and encouragement for what later because my successful attempt, four years later, at becoming president of that same national library association. I could have thought about that earlier experience and decided never to think about running for office again, but I had a reason for wanting to lead the association and to be involved at that level. When I conducted the risk assessment, using the questions above, I believed I had no choice but to move forward with my candidacy. The potential and, in this case, realized, payoff was worth the risk.

Lead

My experiences have afforded me the opportunity to hold leadership positions in academic libraries as well as in library associations. Some of these positions have come with formal titles of leadership (such as committee chair, associate university librarian, and association president). Other positions without these titles have still enabled me to exhibit my ability to lead. Thinking back to the definition of leadership as demonstrating "behavior that influences people toward shared goals," we can see people at all levels of an organization as potential leaders. I reflect on my experiences with my siblings who wanted to emulate the level of freedom I had, or my mentors who encouraged what they believed they saw in me, or my colleagues who supported me along my journey, and I realize that they, too, are leaders. All these people have had a profound impact on my life in leading me down the path I have taken. I have listened attentively, tried to learn a lot, and practiced what I have learned, while also sharing that knowledge with others. These are some of the core qualities I look for in leaders. If asked the question "Are leaders born or made?" I would have to answer "Both!" My experience has certainly been shaped by my experience, but who knows, maybe I was born to lead!

############ REFLECTIONS: KEY LESSONS FOR LEADERS

» Being a leader requires constant growth and development; take advantage of learning opportunities

» Listen to, and learn from, life experiences that have an impact on your ability to lead

» Great leaders encourage and support others who are embarking on their own leadership journey

References

"The Accidental Series." Information Today. http://books.infotoday.com /accidental.shtml (Accessed July 2015).

Figliuolo, Mike. *One Piece of Paper: The Simple Approach to Powerful, Personal Leadership.* San Francisco: Jossey-Bass, 2011.

George, Bill, and Peter Sims. *True North: Discover Your Authentic Leadership.* San Francisco: Jossey-Bass, 2007.

Hernon, Peter, Ronald R. Powell, and Arthur P. Young. *The Next Library Leadership: Attributes of Academic and Public Library Directors.* Westport, CT: Libraries Unlimited, 2003.

Herold, Irene M. H., ed. *Creating Leaders: An Examination of Academic and Research Library Leadership Institutes.* Chicago: Association of College and Research Libraries, 2015.

Pfeiffer, J. William. *The 1995 Annual.* San Diego, CA: Pfeiffer & Company, 1995.

Rost, Joseph C. *Leadership for the Twenty-First Century.* Westport, CT: Praeger Publishers, 1991.

7

NEVER WASTE A GOOD CRISIS: LEADERSHIP IS NOT SUPERVISION AND MORE LESSONS FROM THE CAREER OF A RELUCTANT LEADER

Rosalind Tedford

///////////// **TOP TAKEAWAYS IN THIS CHAPTER**

» Seizing opportunities in a crucible moment can be a hallmark of good leadership

» Leadership and management are not the same thing

» Taking on leadership reluctantly is nothing to fear

» Leaders can learn from watching other leaders during crucible moments

» Not all crucible moments in leadership formation have to happen to you

> Some are born [leaders], some achieve [leadership] and some have [leadership] thrust upon them.
>
> —NOT QUITE SHAKESPEARE, *TWELFTH NIGHT*

I have long had a theory, based primarily on anecdotal experience, that many, if not a majority, of leaders in libraries had their leadership roles thrust upon them rather than actively seeking them out. And many of these took on these leadership roles hesitantly and reluctantly. Library leaders often come up through the ranks, getting promoted, often internally, not because of a desire to lead, but based, they feel, on seniority and skill at their job. Many of the library leaders I know have been these kinds of leaders—taking a chance when it was offered to them, despite their initial unwillingness and their insecurities about their ability to lead people. Often these people fail to realize that they were actually leaders before they were given an official position or supervisory responsibilities that made that leadership role explicit. And these people, once in a position of leadership, may actually continue on to seek leadership roles later in their careers.

Rather than gaining a leadership role that was undeserved, perhaps these leaders were given positions specifically because they had already proven their leadership abilities in an unofficial, nonsupervisory position. I am one of those leaders. My official leadership opportunities have almost always emerged after I have proven myself a leader outside official responsibilities. I have learned about leadership not from having particularly explosive crucible experiences personally but by observing those crucible moments in the life of our university and our library and watching how the leaders handled them. Not all leaders have explicit trials by fire, but most, if not all, have observed these moments and have the opportunities to internalize the lessons they teach about leadership at the turning point.

Leadership Is Not Management

I think there's a tendency to equate leadership with people who manage or supervise other people. Often that is the case. Presidents lead teams of people; CEOs lead teams of people; supervisors lead the people they supervise. Leadership teams in academic libraries are usually formed from the people in management or supervisory positions. But I have come to realize over the course of my 21-year career in libraries that those people in management aren't necessarily all leaders, and the leaders in your library are not all in supervisory positions over others. Often the ability to influence people, to gather people together around a shared project or vision, or even to create trust among a working group are critical qualities for successful leadership. None of these require that the person doing the leading be the supervisor of the people in the group—and often it is to their advantage to have a nonsupervisory role when leading a project. So critical leadership skills are often honed in libraries not by supervising others but by leading in other ways. But it is also often

My official leadership opportunities have almost always emerged after I have proven myself a leader outside official responsibilities.

the case that for many of us, being leaders outside our formal supervisory roles has led to leadership within those roles. That twist on how we emerge as leaders certainly describes my own experience.

My leadership skills were honed not in managing people but in managing processes, projects, and important discussions, both within my library and in the larger university. I had no leadership training of any kind but was a person who naturally tended to think analytically and strategically, and my planning skills were above average. When asked to be on a project team, my inclination was to take charge of the planning and organizing, especially in the absence of anyone else willing or able to do it. My skills in these sorts of situations led me to be seen as someone with "leadership potential," and I was tapped on more than one occasion to step in when a power vacuum arose in our organization. As I took on positions of increasing responsibility in the organization, offered mostly because of my skill at leading projects and processes, I did so hesitantly, even reluctantly. I didn't actively seek out supervisory roles. I set out to help make our library relevant and useful in the larger university, and the supervision followed. In this chapter I want to look at how participating in larger conversations and managing processes can actually be good preparation for more supervisory leadership, especially if those opportunities come as a result of crucible moments.

Learning From a Leader's Crucible Moments

My first full-time library job came as the result of a crucible moment for me that was unrelated to libraries. As I was finishing up my master's thesis in english literature at Wake Forest, I was accepted with a full ride to a doctoral program in Renaissance studies. I went to visit the university, and when I arrived I discovered that the faculty member I had hoped to study with was leaving that institution for another one. On that visit I also got some good advice from a sitting faculty member who cautioned me against pursuing a Ph.D. in an area that was being vociferously cut from many academic programs (my specialty was Shakespeare). I came home and thought long and hard about what I wanted, and I decided that pursuing a Ph.D. was not it. I had to decide what to do. This was, perhaps, my first professional crucible moment—realizing that the plan I had in place for a career wasn't going to happen and deciding what new path I might take.

I had been working in the library as an assistant for the last year of my MA program and really loved the work. Serendipitously, there was a retirement in the department I was working in. My boss offered me the job as a placeholder while I decided how to overcome this crucible moment. I took it. I took it because it felt right, but also because while working in the library, I really came to love the work I was doing and the people I was helping. I was also really good at it. I saw a number of potential changes that could occur if I took the job that would help the department and the library. I really felt like I could be successful and useful—so I said yes. I never imagined that in 20 years I'd be the director of a team of 12 librarians in that very same library.

Not long after I accepted the job, my first real leadership role presented itself, and it happened as my university went through a crucible moment. During my first year of full-time work, Wake Forest had taken an enormous leap of faith and signed a contract with IBM to be the first university in the United States to give laptops to all of its students—this was in 1995. At the time, this was revolutionary, not only in the world of higher education, but it was also a radical change to the day–to-day workings of our very traditional campus. Understandably, and not surprisingly, there was much anxiety all over campus about what changes this decision would bring—to teaching, to learning, and to work processes.

With this anxiety came a good deal of resistance on the part of faculty over the encroachment of technology into their teaching and research. Our library director at the time had participated in meetings about the laptop initiative. She recognized immediately that one way to ease the minds of people was to make sure they were well trained in how to use the new technology. Seeing that her library staff was likely the most computer-savvy group on campus and also recognizing an opportunity for the library to serve as leaders during this time of transition, she volunteered the library to lead the computer training for the project. We would hold training for faculty and staff on their new computers during the summers, and in the fall for students as they got their new computers during orientation. It was an enormous undertaking and a demonstration of how academic library leaders can look for ways to provide their institution with needed services that no one else is delivering. Filling voids like this benefits the campus community and secures the library's place in the mission of the institution.

What I realize in hindsight was that this was a huge leap of faith for the university and our director. The university had to trust that ubiquitous computing was, indeed, the way higher education was heading, and our director had to

I saw the crucible moment for what it was—a game changer— a new direction for both the university and the library, and I felt at my core the need to participate in shaping that new direction.

get her library staff behind the idea of taking on a huge new responsibility. She also had to make sure the training we produced was good enough to alleviate the anxiety and resistance on the larger campus. The library was, in many ways, a neutral player in the decision to offer computers. We weren't seen as part of the administration that many felt were shoving the decision down the throats of the faculty. We were trusted on campus—faculty and students didn't have any negative issues with the library at that point. So having us take on the computer training did, in a way, makes perfect sense if the faculty were going to be brought along into the ubiquitous computing environment that Wake Forest was becoming. But our director's foresight into the importance of this particular moment in time for the university and the library was remarkable. She had no way of knowing then that her leadership decisions at this crucible moment would put the Z. Smith Reynolds (ZSR) Library on the path to being one of the top academic libraries in the country within 15 years.

To make the plan work, the library director needed computer trainers. She looked first to a few of the younger members of the staff, myself among them, asking them to sign on as the core training group. I think she realized that we had more computer experience than some on staff and that we had the energy and excitement needed for the project to be a success. We were too new in our jobs to feel particularly threatened by the new program or to sabotage its success. The entire library staff was under the pressure of needing the program to succeed. My boss saw the potential in me to be a good trainer and he encouraged me to not let the opportunity pass. I was really hesitant to sign on initially because my computer experience was fairly limited and what

I had on it had primarily been on Macintosh computers and the university was going to use PCs.

But my boss had seen me teach people how to use complicated equipment and odd classification schemes from my first day on the job. He said if I could teach someone how to use our microtext machines or understand SuDoc classification, I could teach them how to use computers. He reminded me that it's much harder to teach people to be good teachers than it is to learn a computer system. If I had the first, he said, the second would be the easy part. So I took a leap of faith, along with our director, and signed on to be a trainer. It was scary—it felt like a crucible moment for sure, but it was also exciting. It was his encouragement that gave me the confidence to take the risk.

So I took the step and joined the core training planning and implementation team, and what I found out about myself in the process was that I was a really, really good computer trainer. It wasn't something I had ever thought about career-wise as I was still reeling from my abrupt change of direction after graduate school. Even though I knew only marginally more about computers than the people I taught in those first few sessions, I was really good at planning training—leading training—troubleshooting during class, and easing people's minds about their abilities to learn new things. I had an affinity with the faculty that put them at ease and our training program was very well organized and useful. Maybe more important to my long-term career trajectory, however, what that not only was I good at it but I loved doing it. I felt part of the larger university at this particularly transformative time. I saw faculty's confidence with technology improve, as did our university's reputation for innovation. We were in the national spotlight and I loved being part of that. When the person who was coordinating the training program left for another job on campus, the director asked me to take his job in the library's Information Technology Center. By that time I had finished my MLS degree and was committed to the library as a career path.

I'm not sure I was aware of just how much that personal decision to join the computer training group would change my career, but I was aware that the new laptop program would change the university forever, and I was keenly interested in being part of that evolution. I recognized the chance to be part of the success of the library and the university and I overcame my fears because that was more important to me. I saw the crucible moment for what it was—a game changer—a new direction for both the university and the library, and I felt at my core the need to participate in shaping that new direction. All libraries have staff with similar commitments to moving the library forward, but they approach it differently. Some feel the need to be at the university level, others at the library, or even at their library departmental level. Still others feel the desire for national professional service. I feel strongly that a healthy academic library has people leading at all of those levels—even those not in supervisory positions.

Moving Into Instructional Technology

My next crucible/crisis decision in my career came when, as part of my role in computer training and in leading the ITC, I was asked to be on a committee looking at the new world of course management systems (CMS). The faculty member leading the working group knew me from computer training classes and asked me to be on the team. Our library director, again seeing a turning point for the library in contributing to the university's investigation of new academic technology, encouraged me to join. Unlike my initial hesitancy in taking on computer training, by this point I knew I relished being part of the discussion of these big issues on campus and I readily stepped in.

I found in this committee a knack for keeping projects moving forward, on track, and angled to be successful, and a real love of being at the table when big decisions were being made. I loved the politics of the process. I loved seeing behind the decisions and working with the decision makers. I helped organize the systematic series of questions we put the product through and helped write the final proposal when one was chosen. When we chose the product we wanted and set up a pilot, I ensured that the library was once again put in charge of the training and support for the pilot group. A year later my department (of three) was managing all the training and support for the new CMS.

We were able to leverage the trust that the faculty had developed in us through computer training and parlay it into a widespread adoption and trust among the faculty for this new horizon in teaching and learning. The resistance that had been seen during the laptop program was simply not there for the course management project, and a large reason for that, I believe, was that by then the faculty trusted the library not to lead them astray when it came to technology—if we were behind it and supporting it, the faculty would listen. Our leadership during the crucible of the launch of the laptop program reaped rewards in widespread adoption of this new academic technology.

Although not as radical an event as the laptop project, Wake Forest's adoption of a course management system was still a big step for the university. At that point in time, Wake Forest had invested heavily in an expensive, home-grown system for a couple of years through Lotus Notes. Championed by our then provost, the "Wake Forest template," as we had called it, was touted by him as the next big thing for us, and he even had plans to package it and offer it to other institutions. This homegrown system had cost a lot to develop and unfortunately created a fair amount of frustration on the part of the faculty because the platform was unstable and was often off-line when needed most. We in the Information Technology Center had been doing the training on that system and knew that it was an idea before its time and was ultimately unsustainable. Recognizing that the future of academic technology likely led through course management systems, and also conceding that ours was not going to work out, our provost decided to investigate replacements for "the template." From this crucible moment and his handling of it, I learned that when facing problems, leaders may have to abandon initial ideas (even when they are attached to them) and must regroup and try again. Calling it quits on something he believed so much in and allowing us to investigate commercial packages was certainly a crucible moment for him, but he was willing to do it for the good of the university's mission.

Soon after joining the CMS group, the head of the Information Technology Center where I worked left, and the library director immediately wanted to promote me into that position. I thought it was a classic case of the Peter Principle being put into action. It was, in some ways, a logical step for me, but it was my first job with official professional staff supervisory expectations (I had managed a few student assistants over the years) and that was a real challenge. But by that time I learned where my skill set really lay, and had also learned that I liked being in on important, university-wide conversations too much to turn the job down. Even so, I was concerned about my managerial role. While I had been a successful leader of projects, I was less sure about my skills in leading a department. I was good at managing processes, coordinating projects, creating course outlines, even steering conversations, but I was nervous and reluctant to take on the direct supervision of people, especially coworkers. But there was no one else to do it, and bringing someone in from the outside to head up a unit that was so ingrained with current Wake Forest–specific projects seemed untenable at the time. So I said yes.

So in six years I went from a graduate assistant to manager of the department responsible for all computer training on campus, all because in a crucible moment, our university took a chance, our director took a chance, and I took a chance. There was no competition for either of the jobs in the Information Technology Center—I was tapped based purely on my success as a trainer in the program up to that point. My skill at leading projects, honed by watching a great director at work and strengthened by working with other library leaders who encouraged and mentored me along the way, ultimately led to an opportunity to lead as a manager. In hindsight it should not have been such a tough decision—leadership is often confused with management, and what the first six years of my career should have taught me is that leadership and management are separate things. You can lead without having any direct reports and you can manage without being a great leader. I had clearly proven myself capable of leadership by coordinating the training program and participating in the CMS project. I was, as of yet, untested in the supervisory role and feared that my skill in one would not translate to skill in the other. I guess when progressing from a position to leadership outside supervision to leadership with supervisory duties, the sweet spot is learning to combine the two. Some days I feel like I'm still looking to combine the two.

From Management Back to Leadership

After securing the library's place as the leader of technology implementation and training on campus, our director continued to make good decisions in crucible moments. In 2002, once again trying to ensure our library's place in the work of the campus, she saw the increasing interest in the library profession in information literacy in the college curriculum and asked the

Leadership is often confused with management, and what the first six years of my career should have taught me is that leadership and management are separate things.

reference librarians to develop a for-credit Information Literacy class. At this point, our librarians had only ever done typical one-shot bibliographic instruction, never a for-credit class. As you might imagine, there was some skepticism and push-back. But the director clearly saw direct participation in the teaching mission of the university as a way to increase the relevance of the library in an increasingly digital world. It wasn't a particularly popular decision on her part. It was tasked to the Reference Department with no allowance for the time it would take to teach and no additional compensation offered to the librarians who would be teaching.

It was a top-down directive and it didn't sit well with all of the librarians on the team. Top-down directives often backfire and create long-term resentment, and, in hindsight, she probably should have let it bubble up from below, but in this case it likely never would have. The director wanted the library to become more enmeshed with the teaching mission of the university. She thought that teaching for-credit classes was how we would move from being perceived as simply a service unit on campus to being seen as educational partners on par with faculty. With the advent of the Internet, the value and relevance of libraries for the future of higher education was being questioned. Her desire to make that question moot on our campus resulted in a rather rare top-down directive. Despite the reluctance surrounding its inception, our for-credit class did prove to be the next big decision that positioned ZSR as a library admired for its leadership both on campus and nationally.

The mandate to create what is now called LIB100, however, proved to be one of our director's last big endeavors at ZSR, as she passed away suddenly in 2003 during the summer, after seeing only two pilot classes taught. With our participation in the laptop and CMS projects, combined with the development of our for-credit class, our library director started our library down the path for long-term relevance and reverence on campus. I often wonder if she saw what she was doing at that time. Our success with training and support for the laptop and CMS projects served to give the library a privileged place on campus in terms of gaining faculty and staff trust—something we learned to rely on and continued to actively develop as time went on. Her gambles paid off, but they were still huge gambles. Her absence left the library in a bit of a crucible moment of its own. The sudden loss of our director made for a rough year. By summer 2004 we hired a new director, and she taught me a good deal more about leadership through crucible moments.

As we were just at the beginning of our for-credit information literacy course, I had been recruited to the development team to help develop the curriculum for copyright and plagiarism. As the course progressed, I found I was more and more interested in teaching not just the copyright classes but my own complete sections. I was able to do this in spring 2004 when the head of reference left the university, thus leaving two sections without an instructor. I volunteered. As the semester wore on I realized that this kind of in-depth information literacy instruction felt like the natural next step for me. I liked being tied to the overall instruction mission of the university and loved being part of the beginning of this new step for ZSR. But it was hard to commit to teaching the class long-term in the position I held, so when our new director was hired, I took another risk.

The departure of the head of reference had left a joint Head of Reference/Information Literacy Librarian position open. I had never worked in our Reference Department and was reluctant to take the helm there, so I had not applied. I was also reluctant because I still didn't feel like supervision was my strength, and that position had five direct reports under it at the time. However, the Information Literacy portion of the job appealed to me. After a failed initial search to find someone to fill that job, I decided to take a chance and e-mail our new director in fall 2004 to say that I would be very interested in the position of Information Literacy Librarian but not in the Head of Reference part of the job, if that could be worked out. Surprisingly, the director agreed to it. She said something along the lines of "I have learned to do what it takes to keep good employees happy." She reworked the position and created a Reference Coordinator position that would rotate through the existing Reference Librarians as a way to avoid having a head of the department. She then appointed me as the Information Literacy Librarian.

I won't lie—part of what appealed to me about that job was that I got to go back to being a worker-bee—no direct reports. I could lead this fledgling information literacy program and see it grow without having to supervise people. Continuing to build my project management skills, I spent the next few years turning our three sections of Info Lit (IL) class per semester into a full-blown program that now fills 15 to 18 sections a semester. I developed a course template, and with the blessing of our new director, recruited more librarians from other departments to teach and arranged for IL instruction to be listed on the job description of most of the librarians we hired. While none of these librarians reported directly to me, I was the leader of this program, and it was remarkably successful.

Leading and Managing

Within a short period I returned to a supervisory position. The rotating Reference Coordinator position rotated through the other two people in the department willing to take it on for a year each, but none of the other librarians in the department wanted it. The shared leadership model was unsustainable when so few were willing. Despite the fact that the team had enthusiastically agreed to the proposal when it was first presented to them, when it actually came time to volunteer to be the next year's coordinator, most declined. And so, before long I was asked to step into the leadership vacuum as the permanent Assistant Director for Reference. At that point our Reference and Technology teams were combined under one director and I would be the Assistant Director for Research and Instruction. There was a parallel Assistant Director for Technology and we both reported to the same director. The transition to supervisor was a fairly easy one as I had already been a de facto leader of the group as far as the information literacy class was concerned. There were no other internal candidates and members of the department seemed genuinely happy to have someone more permanent take the helm. Still, I was unconvinced of my supervisory skills, but I knew that being in the permanent role would give me access to discussions at a higher level, both within the library and the larger university, and that made it seem worthwhile to me.

From this new leadership position I was able to observe the university and the library through more crucible moments. The library director turned out to be particularly good at spotting these moments and making the most of them. She was another leader who saw the potential in the important turning points of the institution and forged her legacy in the crucible moments. When students begged for the library to be open longer hours, she shifted money around to make us 24/5. When we got a new provost who encouraged her to pursue faculty status for librarians as a way to keep us in line with the university's mission, she guided us expertly through that process—becoming a dean herself. When the university made the tough decision to bring in more students to increase revenue, the dean helped ensure that the library benefitted with major renovations, including the addition of a Starbucks and more student study space. When the finances of the university suffered during the economic downturn of 2008 to 2010, she used it as a catalyst to cancel print journals and save the library significant money. Her motto, shared with our forward-thinking provost at the time, became "never waste a good crisis." And the result of her leadership was that she created a library that was good enough to win the 2011 ACRL Excellence in Academic Libraries award. As part of the second tier of leadership in the library during these events, I watched her and learned some of the big lessons of leadership.

Three years later I was asked to become a director when the Assistant Director for Technology left and our director was promoted to associate dean. Our dean decided to recruit a Director of Technology and asked me to take the job as Director for Research and Instruction. In some ways I felt like I didn't have a choice, but in reality I took the job because the success of the library was so important to me that I felt it was time to step up and officially take on the leadership position that many thought I had unofficially occupied for most of my career. When I took that position, the department had six people—we have since doubled in size. I'm still not always comfortable with the supervisory aspects of the role but am now engaged in discussions at all areas of the university and am seen as an essential partner to consult when complex issues arise on campus. I've made a kind of peace with my place as a leader, and while I still often wonder about the supervisory aspects of the job, I feel much less ambivalent about the benefits of leadership.

Conclusion

My leadership crucibles have mainly been personal crucibles, deciding whether to take official leadership roles. But my thinking about leadership has been formed in large part by watching great leaders as they lead during rough times. Seeing leaders take chances when the library or the institution is going through a crucible moment has led me to understand the reality of not wasting a good crisis. Taking chances and going down "the road less traveled" is not only visionary but can pave the way for really great things to come. As a result of watching good leaders lead good people through transformative experiences, I am very attuned to the opportunities that change provides. I now think less about the negatives during a crisis or crucible and focus on how to rethink the possibilities. Crucibles will happen. It's how we respond to them that defines us as leaders.

REFLECTIONS: KEY LESSONS FOR LEADERS

» If you have an area of weakness, such as supervision, work with a mentor to build your skills and confidence levels

» Pay attention to what other leaders do, both good and bad; it contributes to your growth as a leader

» Identify who the reluctant leaders are in your organization and determine how you can help them to emerge and develop as a leader

» Keep an eye on and an ear out for the larger library and institutional environment for crucible moments in the making; being at the table in these moments can make all the difference for your own library

— 8 —

ON BECOMING: THE TEN-THOUSAND-HOUR JOURNEY TOWARD POSITIVE LEADERSHIP

Jon E. Cawthorne

///////////// **TOP TAKEAWAYS IN THIS CHAPTER**

» Be the captain of your own career; don't wait for others to create opportunities

» Take calculated risks, but self-growth will accelerate learning

» Always remember, you need every experience to reach your potential

> Waking up to who you are requires letting go of who you imagine yourself to be.
>
> —ALAN WATTS

Malcolm Gladwell, in his book *Outliers: The Story of Success*, describes the amount of time it takes to achieve success in any field. Gladwell believes that those who are considered successful spend over 10,000 hours honing their craft. Any discussion of leadership should begin with this insight. Most people know that within those 10,000 hours, failures will happen. As with professionals in many fields, librarians rise to leadership positions through excellence, investment of time and effort, and success in operational levels of the organization. This means that the time spent serving and learning in leadership roles may be only the beginning of the 10,000-hour journey toward mastery. In the context of preparing for a leadership position, you might very well start your 10,000 hours by reading this book, watching and learning from others, or thinking deeply about your own personal development.

The story of my experience is one of ambition, self-reflection and growth, and, finally, gratitude.

At the outset of the 10,000 hours of becoming a leader, you will need to ask yourself some critical questions: Where does your interest to lead come from? Why do you see yourself in leadership positions? What leadership lessons can you learn from your current experiences? How many new insights can you learn from communicating with and leading other people? Has failure factored into your learning and influenced your actions? To what extent has greater self-awareness played a part in your own growth? The goal of this chapter is to share my answers to these questions and provide the inspiration for aspiring leaders to recognize that the leadership path is a long journey but that the work can be extremely rewarding. The story of my experience is one of ambition, self-reflection and growth, and, finally, gratitude for finally arriving as the Dean of Libraries.

A person cannot become a truly inspiring leader without personal reflection, growth, and transformation. My own learning over the course of a 22-year career has given me the necessary experiences, both positive and negative, to be able to grow, rethink, and develop a positive vision. While there is a certain level of risk stepping into any organization, taking on new projects, or advocating innovation, experiencing failure along the way is meaningless if real learning does not follow. The good news is that everyone can become a leader. I can't say I have mastered it yet, but I am deeply grateful for each and every failure and stumble, large and small.

In the world of research librarianship, a great need exists to communicate positively about the future. Yes, there are many uncertainties. New developments in technology, changing economies related to scholarly communication, and creating and communicating a vision are all extremely challenging. Jim Kouzes and Barry Posner, founders of the Leadership Challenge, understand that the key for leaders is their credibility. In their Five Practices of Exemplary Leadership Model, Kouzes and Posner share the following set of starting points for those who wish to achieve Positive Leadership:

» Model the way
» Inspire a shared vision

» Challenge the process
» Enable others to act
» Encourage the heart

This description of the five practices of exemplary leaders, and the concept of exemplary leadership itself, are ideals, yet considering these points in the context of current library leaders, one can then ask: Do they meet or exceed this description? Why or why not? If a leader does something exceptionally well, is he or she able to share his or her approach and thinking? Beginning a leadership journey requires a consideration of what current leaders are accomplishing and how they are doing it, and examining this set of practices is an excellent place to begin. If you find leaders who meet these five criteria, I can assure you that their libraries are doing exceptionally well under the stewardship of a Positive Leader. From my experience, using these five practices, not only can you can recognize a good leader but it can serve as an equally good starting path on the road to exemplary leadership.

Deciding to Pursue a Leadership Position

When I started thinking about working in this profession, I envisioned myself at the reference desk in a public library, the people's university. Leading or working in a research library was not on my radar. I was fortunate to receive an internship in library administration within a public library. I started my professional career at Ohio State University Libraries. It was a two-year, minority librarian internship. Often professionals, especially early in their careers, enter organizations in one single position. This internship/residency position was a tremendous gift because it allowed me to move around to different positions, gaining experience and perspective across, up, and down the organization. After rotating through all the areas of a major research library, I selected a focus on reference and East Asian studies.

I recall the exact moment I decided to gain the experience necessary to compete for library dean or university librarian jobs. I sat in the library dean's office, and he asked me, "Jon, what do you want to do in your career?" I said, "You know, I think I want to do what you do!" I will never forget his comment: "No, you don't want to become a library director; you want to become a department head in a research library. They have a lot of influence and get things done." I remember leaving his office, thinking and promising myself that I would make it my career goal to become a library director. It was in this position that I asked myself: Who makes decisions in these organizations? Why and how are decisions communicated? Why are sentiments of low morale and lack of communication so common?

As I thought about my career, I had an expectation of what being in the top position would be like. I thought I knew about leadership. I thought I knew myself. Turns out I didn't know much about either. When I started, I thought I knew everything and that the path to library leadership was simply about acquiring all the right skills and abilities. What was quite unexpected, and constantly surprises me, was the depth and complexity of leadership positions. These positions are not solely about books, electronic resources, or library values—they are about people. What do all library employees experience in the current environment? How does a leader inspire people? Not only does a leader need the right skills and abilities, but also, to be truly effective, I believe every leader needs substantive internal growth and considerable struggle toward self-understanding.

The absence of this internal work affects a person's ability to lead with emotional intelligence, develop character, empathize, communicate, and articulate an inspiring vision; these are qualities that are universally accepted in successful leadership positions in all industries. Much of what I have experienced, both positive and negative, particularly in the last several library leadership positions I've held, has caused me to become much more humble about what I think I know. I know I don't have it all figured out, but just as I did the difficult internal work to understand who I am and where I want to go, I've become quite passionate about creating an inclusive organization for people and communicating more positively about the amazing future we have in academic libraries. I certainly ask a lot of questions to identify, understand, and influence change within the organizational culture.

I thought I knew about leadership. I thought I knew myself. Turns out I didn't know much about either.

I was idealistic enough to believe that librarians help people find the information they need to make better decisions in their lives. Even with greater access to the Internet, an important opportunity remains for our profession: to help people sift through all of the information and help them know what they don't know. Yet, while there is instant gratification in assisting people at the desk, I realized that library administration represented an even greater opportunity to influence the entire culture of an organization. My interest then spread to the professional association.

Finding a Leadership Role Outside the Library

My desire to lead evolved gradually. Like many new librarians, I was somewhat overwhelmed by the committee structure of the American Library Association. The possibilities seemed endless. At this point in my career, I decided to seek out leaders in the profession—people who were administering major academic and public libraries. As I met with many of them, I began to see some common threads. These leaders believed their work wasn't about money or status—instead what came across was their deep passion for libraries. They were all extremely encouraging. While they never mentioned their particular organizational or staffing challenges, it was clear that they relied on a deeper understanding of leadership within libraries than I had previously encountered. So although I lacked the context at that point to fully understand the advice they offered or the work they were accomplishing, I appreciated their encouragement and continued to pursue leadership training as a way to prepare myself for the future.

My leadership development training expanded my concept of what it meant to become a leader. Some training sessions helped me explore my personal leadership style. Other programs, panels, and activities were designed to assess each person's leadership within a group. Ultimately, I participated in Snowbird Leadership Institute, Emerging Leaders, ARL/Leadership Career Development, and Senior Fellows. Programs of this type help future leaders become more self-aware and they also help each participant build a professional network.

One professional development session stood out above the rest. A dean of libraries gave a presentation on "A Day in the Life of a Dean." This dean began by outlining how the day might start: with an e-mail from a staff member, a call from the president's office, and a meeting with the office of general counsel. She spoke specifically about her leadership philosophy for prioritizing each of these and the political implications of her approach and outcomes. What struck me was how many different ways there were to achieve resolution, to problem-solve, build confidence, communicate, and energize people in the organization. This was a pivotal moment in my thinking. My leadership experience up to that point had been primarily theoretical, and this was the first time I had given serious thought to what the work of a library leader might actually look like. In fact, I was participating in so many leadership development opportunities during that period that one mentor asked me, "Well, when are you going to lead?"

As I started my career, I had no idea of the extent to which I was going to grow and change. If individuals want to pursue leadership, they should learn from examples all around us, both good and bad. I think people follow leaders they respect. Leaders who promote division, fear, and control only last so long. If a library leader is asking everyone in the organization to consider new opportunities, I wonder how comfortable and flexible that leader is with change? I think a critical skill is the courage to act, but also to listen, and to understand that the work of leadership is about changing the current culture.

After rising to leadership positions, has the internal work resulted in the maturity to accept people around them telling the truth? Because I've been in many organizations and gone through a great deal of self-reflection, I am convinced the path to a sustainable, compelling, inclusive, and inspiring vision requires internal work and growth. I can honestly say that I'm a different person than when I started, but I'm looking forward to learning, growing, and constantly reconsidering what I think I know.

A Traumatic, Shaky Start

If a leadership position is an aspiration, these questions will inevitably come up: When is the right time to lead? Where? How? I began reviewing job advertisements for leaders. As I read the ads, I paid particular attention to the skills and abilities I wanted to develop: budget, personnel, facilities, and development. These all required common, overlapping skills, and in my current position in an academic library, I was making little progress toward gaining them. As much as I wanted to be in higher-level positions, I still needed people to believe in me. Around this time I had the opportunity to leave academic libraries and become the director of a main library within a large public library. This was a huge change. It was also a risk that people could not really understand my choice, which made me question my decision. My colleagues in academic libraries said I would never be able to return, but I was still uncertain that following a traditional academic career path would result in leading a research library.

In my first day as a manager, I had to quickly learn employment contracts, facilities issues, budget, and all personnel policies and procedures. Those were straightforward enough, but in addition to learning everything about the job, I was also presented with long-time employees and a new organizational culture. For leaders at any level, a clear understanding of how the culture works is an important indicator of what can be accomplished, especially early on. My introduction to the library culture came in the form of union grievances. The filing of grievances can be the library manager's bane of existence. The grievance process allows union members to file a formal protest when they believe an action by management violates their bargaining agreement. In many ways, union grievances represent the best way for employees to communicate with management.

During my tenure in the public library, grievances represented the accepted way to communicate with library administration. In my first year I received many, many grievances. As a newly hired manager, I needed to ask many questions about the service delivered at this library. One of my first inquiries resulted in a grievance. The question seemed simple. Why, I asked, if the library opens at 8:00 A.M., do staff show up to work the desk at 9:30 A.M.? This was a reasonable question, but each grievance represented some kind of miscommunication and failure. As a new manager I had an insufficient understanding of how best to communicate with staff and their union stewards. This was a major problem. I also lacked an overall strategy for change, and, since communication was poor, I didn't know how to involve the right people in decision making.

Another memorable failure came when I hired my first professional librarian. This was a misstep, because within six months of the person's hire, I had to let this individual go due to poor job performance. Eventually, I learned how to communicate more effectively. I became acquainted with the organization's influential leaders. Ultimately, I realized that through careful communication, listening, and empathy, I was able to make changes in a highly unionized library environment. I also began to use the informal communication channels that were already present. In retrospect, I am convinced the risk I took in leaving my reference position was the right decision, because this nonacademic management post prepared me for better things to come.

Developing: The Path to Personal Growth

My next challenge was moving from a large, public library back to an academic library. Normally, this is not a recommended path because of the way academic libraries hire. Yet with all the management experience I had acquired in the public library, I was able to return to an academic library in the role of Associate University Librarian for Information and Collections. One of the first decisions I needed to make in my next place of employment was to hire a staff member to work an information desk that was less than 10 feet from the reference desk. After consulting widely, I decided not to hire a person for that post. I was called to a meeting with many staff and library faculty who were upset by the decision. I listened carefully and then said, recalling my time at another library, that I obviously didn't understand what happens between the information desk and the reference desk, so I agreed to work on both in the coming year. Further, I said, I would ask for volunteers to work the information desk.

During that year, I worked on both the reference desk and information desks. Eighteen months later, librarians, staff members, and I worked together to combine the two desks into one. Much later, several staff members and librarians who had opposed the move came to agree with it. This was definitely a crucible moment. Sometimes leaders must stand firm and make what might seem like an unpopular decision in the short term. I admit making a decision like this with such a short tenure in the organization was particularly challenging. However, I gained a great deal of resolve considering how to reorganize the staff under a new service desk model. Further, by personally working the desk for a year and asking for volunteers to staff the information desk, I demonstrated that I wanted to understand the dynamic between the two desks.

I have come to believe that personal growth— through the cycle of risk, failure, and the new understandings that arise from both of these—is at the core of developing a vision and becoming a successful and inspiring leader.

As this moment from my career demonstrates, difficult decisions rarely become any less stressful or complicated. Even after widely consulting others and asking all the right questions, a leader may still feel like his or her final decision was an ill-advised choice. A leader must trust that with a longer arc, these decisions will prove beneficial to the organization, the department, and the students. In my career, I've made some difficult decisions but they always managed to resolve successfully. Demonstrating confidence in one's decisions should never lead to a mentality that one's actions are always the right path. That type of hubris eventually brings on a leader's downfall. Passing through this crucible led to a personal transition that fostered my personal growth as I sought similar or higher-level positions.

Anyone interested in library administration will at some point spend a good deal of time in personal reflection. My 10,000 hours consisted of time spent as a library administrator in several different institutions. As I finished my advanced degree, I reflected on my own accomplishments, miscommunications, and aborted projects and plans. During this time, I gained experience through multiple senior leadership positions. My personal development accelerated, however, when I attended a leadership program that allowed visits to a number of different academic libraries. Each of them featured an opportunity, along with my cohort colleagues, to meet with provosts and presidents. Hearing the leadership stories of these most senior academic administrators proved a useful learning experience. Hearing their stories reminded me about the challenges of effective communication, staff development, and organizational change.

Reflections on Personal Growth

My journey, although far from complete, is rife with examples of gradual learning, listening for facts that fit what I believed, and allowing crises and failures to guide me in letting go of many earlier versions of myself. In fact, I have come to believe that personal growth—through the cycle of risk, failure, and the new understandings that arise from both of these—is at the core of developing a vision and becoming a successful and inspiring leader. There is great debate about whether a leader is born or made. I think everyone has the potential for leadership. For some people (and I would fall into this category), it may take working in several organizations to develop the qualities necessary to fully realize that potential.

A person interested in leadership might ask: What level of risk am I comfortable with? How many failures and stumbles must I have? How can I develop a compelling vision? As leaders ask their organizations to change, I would ask: How comfortable is the leader with change? Is it possible to relate or empathize with people in the organization?

Of course, what happens over time through listening, questioning, and initiating many changes is that one gets better at all of these—back to the 10,000 hours. Taking risks and asking the difficult questions at each stage is vital for both recognizing crucible moments and emerging stronger, ready for the next challenge.

No matter what stage of a career journey you may be in, the 10,000 hours of learning to bring about sustainable change and become a genuinely inspiring leader must include an abiding interest in people, a great deal of humility, and an ever-adjusting sense of self-awareness. One cannot become an inspiring leader without taking risks and making many false steps, but I can think of few professions more worth the sacrifice. For most who aspire to become leaders, the inevitable failures bring opportunities for greater self-awareness, correction, reflection, and ultimately for creating and being able to communicate a positive and inspiring vision. As a staff member or professional at any level, I am able to enjoy success in my work only if it is based on both the investment of time spent by talented leaders and the work those leaders are willing to undertake to get to the core of who they are. Have you woken up to who you are?

////////// REFLECTIONS: KEY LESSONS FOR LEADERS

» Dedicate time to learn the craft of leadership with people, projects, and time in reflection

» A leadership journey is equal parts external (what people see) and internal (what people don't see)

» Leadership is about listening, flexibility, and empowerment, and much less about control and imposing one's will over others

References

Arbinger Institute. *Leadership and Self-Deception: Getting Out of the Box.* San Francisco: Berrett-Koehler, 2002.

Bolman, Lee G., and Terrence E. Deal. *Reframing Organizations: Artistry, Choice, and Leadership.* Jossey-Bass Business and Management Series. San Francisco: Jossey-Bass, 2008.

Boyatzis, Richard E., and Annie McKee. *Resonant Leadership: Renewing Yourself and Connecting With Others Through Mindfulness, Hope, and Compassion.* Cambridge, MA: Harvard Business School Press, 2005.

Cooperrider, David L., and Diana Whitney. *Appreciative Inquiry: A Positive Revolution in Change.* San Francisco: Berrett-Koehler, 2005.

Gladwell, Malcolm. *Outliers: The Story of Success.* Boston: Little, Brown and Company, 2008.

Jamison, Kaleel. *The Nibble Theory and the Kernel of Power: A Book About Leadership, Self-Empowerment, and Personal Growth.* New York: Paulist, 1984.

Kouzes, James M., and Barry Z. Posner. *The Leadership Challenge: How to Get Extraordinary Things Done in Organizations.* Jossey-Bass Business and Management Series. San Francisco: Jossey-Bass, 2012.

Schein, Edgar H. *Organizational Culture and Leadership,* 4th ed. San Francisco: Jossey-Bass, 2010.

Watkins, Michael D. *The First 90 Days: Critical Success Strategies for New Leaders at all Levels.* Cambridge, MA: Harvard Business School Press, 2003.

Wheatley, Margaret J. *Leadership and the New Science: Learning About Organization From an Orderly Universe.* San Francisco: Berrett-Koehler, 1992.

Wheatley, Margaret J., and Myron Kellner-Rogers. *A Simpler Way.* San Francisco: Berrett-Koehler, 1996.

9

LEADERSHIP WHERE YOU MIGHT OVERLOOK IT: OPPORTUNITY CALLS AT A COMMUNITY COLLEGE

José A. Aguiñaga

////////////// TOP TAKEAWAYS IN THIS CHAPTER

>> Engage actively at the local, state, and national levels

>> Demonstrate your skills with any formal or informal opportunities

>> Showcase your professionalism at all times by your actions and words

>> Go beyond the status quo, demonstrate your proactive engagement

>> Remain humble and never be arrogant even if you feel you're right

>> Saying yes to an unexpected opportunity may create a path to greater responsibility as a leader

How I Got Here

Prior to beginning my community college librarian career, the first half of my academic librarian experiences had taken place at various university libraries in Arizona, California, and Texas. During the first 10-plus years of my career, I gained numerous experiences that would benefit my transition to the community college. The progress of my academic librarian career began at a pivotal point during the dissemination of online information—the launching of Internet browsers. I vividly recall using Mosaic.1 The Internet would be a key variable in the future of libraries and librarians. Completing my Master of Library Science degree from the University of Arizona and beginning to interview for academic librarian positions led me to wonder where I would go and what my first professional job as a librarian would be. During the latter part of my graduation semester, I was offered a temporary social sciences librarian position at the University of Houston Libraries. Why did I take this

There are times when all leaders need to be risk takers. The reward may be less clear at the beginning but it will eventually become obvious as you continue with your career and personal life.

temporary job? Now that I reflect on this event, it came down to a few reasons. The opportunity to begin a new career and learn from a positive work environment was a primary factor, and second, my intuition was telling me to take a chance. There are times when all leaders need to be risk takers. The reward may be less clear at the beginning but it will eventually become obvious as you continue with your career and personal life.

What I gained in experience while working at the University of Houston has proven to be my foundation as a professional librarian. Being given a chance to demonstrate my contributions with unexpected situations was rewarding. For example, after one year as a social sciences librarian, I was summoned by the associate dean to become the interim library personnel director. I was unsure why I was selected but I believe it was because of the professionalism that I demonstrated during my initial year in Houston. In the next two years, I led and coordinated all librarian hiring, recruitment, hiring committee oversight, salary negotiation, compliance with human resources policies and regulations, and many other personnel-related tasks. This was my first true leadership experience.

Leading a university library's personnel department, and learning from the numerous occasions when I made mistakes, became an eye-opening initial experience as an academic librarian. One incident in particular, when I had to finalize my initial librarian recruitment search without the guidance of my direct supervisor, stands out in my mind as a crucible moment. My supervisor was ill that day, and with a pending deadline, I had to make a decision without the benefit of a consultation. Having the opportunity to lead, but also to pause and learn from my missteps, was paramount to my professional development. This leadership foundation was built with assistance from many colleagues during the first half of my academic librarian career. Leaving the University of Houston was difficult. The main reason I left Houston was personal. I sorely missed living in my hometown of San Diego. Early in 1997, I became aware of a librarian opportunity at my undergraduate alma mater. Returning back home and to my undergraduate institution was ideal.

The professional and personal relationships that I developed in Houston eased the transition. What made it better was the ease of staying in touch and reconnecting with them during the progression of my career.

As I continued in my career as an academic librarian at other universities, having the ability to continue to grow personally and professionally became fundamental to my development and experience with leadership opportunities at a formal or informal stage. After leaving Houston, I would continue to gain other experiences while residing in Phoenix, Arizona, and San Diego and Long Beach, California. Here is an example from my time at California State University, Long Beach. While working at this institution, colleagues advised me to get involved with the faculty union and pursue my second masters. These colleagues challenged me to grow as a leader through formal and informal educational opportunities.

I made the decision to run for the library representative and also decided to begin my master of public administration (MPA) program. Both decisions would become the foundation for what I would experience in the near future. Serving the needs of my constituents was key to accepting this new leadership role. Having the ability to communicate the needs and wants of my union sisters and brothers was important to me. With a new understanding of the organizational culture of this institution as a leader and as a student learning from my MPA courses, I was gaining a better understanding of the academy. From this leadership experience, I learned to be ready for change and growth as a professional.

The key variables to my contributions in my leadership experiences are to remain calm and definitely to listen. It is more important to listen than talk when communicating. One thing I have learned is knowing when to intervene in a situation to promote a workable solution. The combination of opportunities within the first half of my career has elevated my level of participation within community college institutions.

Transitioning to a Community College

I eventually decided to leave the university environment. At the time, I was not sure why I made the decision, but it has become clearer to me in recent years. I am beginning my 11th year as a community college faculty librarian and certainly do not regret the transition from the university to a two-year institution. I have found many reasons to appreciate this decision to change my career path.

During the first 10 years of my community college career, change happened at many levels, beginning with my relocation back to Arizona in 2005. I had been accepted into the public administration doctoral program at Arizona State University. The reason I applied for this doctoral program was the intellectual stimulation that I gained from my MPA degree at California State University, Long Beach. Understanding and discussing the academic discourse of public administration with professors stimulated my pursuit of understanding the theoretical nature of this field. Additionally, by applying for this doctoral program, my plan was to position myself for advancement in librarianship.

Even though I attended classes for only two semesters and eventually withdrew from the program, what I gained most from this experience was to rethink what I wanted to do as a professional. My wife, who is also a librarian, provided me with valuable insights and poignant questions as to why I needed to continue with work and pursue the doctoral degree. This crucible moment provided me an opportunity to deeply reflect on my professional goals, and that was to become an academic library administrator. What did I learn from this moment in my life? Never give up on your goals. Sometimes the pursuit of your goals may take longer than you think. If that's the case, there's a reason. In due time, all will make sense to you as a professional and person.

Recalling this moment from 2005 makes me understand that as library professionals, we need to find varied types of intellectual stimulation so we do not become bored with what we are doing at work. By pursuing additional education, whether it is another degree or professional development courses, you discover and refine new interests that could make you a better academic administrator or a more insightful leader. So with all of this in mind, during my last two years in Long Beach, I started and completed my Master of Public Administration degree. I was intrigued by what I could do with a doctoral degree. As a first-generation Latino, completing my second master's degree was a feat in itself, but pondering whether I should pursue a doctoral program was a tall order. Besides relocating to Arizona and pursuing the doctorate in public administration, I also needed to be employed, and that's where the complete transition would evolve. I was hired by one of the 10 Maricopa community colleges, Glendale Community College (GCC). This college serves over 18,000 students and has served the northwest valley in the Phoenix area for the past 50 years. So my relocation to Arizona was twofold in purpose—work and education.

Initially at GCC

Acclimating to the library and college organizational culture was paramount to understanding the modus operandi of the past, present, and future of GCC. After my initial year and after conversations with seasoned faculty colleagues, it dawned on me that greater opportunities and experiences would be waiting in the not-so-distant future. After withdrawing from the doctoral program at Arizona State University, I decided to refocus my energies and attention on my academic librarian career. I learned that paying attention to my work at GCC and immersing myself in it enabled me to advance to the next phase of my career. Contributing to the intellectual, cultural, and social life of my library and college gave me the opportunity to demonstrate my value as an academic librarian to faculty, administrators, and—best of all—to the students and members of the community who frequented our library. Seeing the aspirations of community members developing and making a change in their lives has made everything worthwhile. Still, I continued to explore different doctoral programs and wondered if I should take on a new challenge to advance my career.

Transitioning from dual roles as academic librarian and doctoral student to solely a librarian was crucial to what would come next regarding my leadership opportunities. Engaging with my primary duties as a faculty librarian gave me time to reflect and contribute to the fine work of the library. Providing assistance at the reference desk, giving instruction in numerous subject areas, and overseeing the online library research resources aided in my development as a contributor and leader. Being the college's faculty lead for selecting and acquiring library research resources nourished my growth as a leader. Overseeing the daily maintenance of our online library resources became a task that grew exponentially when our library director informed me of additional funds that were available to purchase a greater number of online tools. This task provided me a chance to collaborate, consult, and analyze which online resources our library and students could use. Understanding the data from this analysis process enlightened the recommendations that I would provide to library colleagues for consideration. Leading the library in acquiring new online resources was definitely instrumental in fostering my belief that I could take on more leadership responsibility in the library.

My leadership role became evident in being the bridge between my library faculty colleagues and vendors. Maintaining good relations with vendors, whether their products were selected for purchase or not, was important. A bit of diplomacy came into play while demonstrating my leadership skills to my colleagues and the vendors. Once a final decision was made, I contacted each vendor and thanked them for their time and dedication in assisting our library, even if their product was not chosen. For the past eight years, I have been the assigned librarian who oversees the acquisition, maintenance, and negotiation with vendors. During this time, I have had a few instances that tested my ability to manage relationships between my library faculty colleagues and vendors. I recall one time when a vendor was cold-calling one of my colleagues and had made arrangements to have a database trial, without sharing this information with me. After being informed by other colleagues of this situation, I engaged in a conversation with my colleague, library director, and then the vendor about future database trials. I believe this manifests the acceptance of my professional judgment and leadership in providing access to tools that are available 24/7 for all library users at GCC. This primary job assignment has also expanded my level of contributions to the college.

Committees

At GCC, library faculty are primarily responsible for effective teaching but also serve on college or district-wide committees each academic year. Most of the time, each faculty is assigned from two to three committees per academic year. My first assignment was the college assessment committee. I served as a member for six years. During this time, it was definitely intriguing to understand how the college was adhering to the higher education assessment culture. Our college has primary and secondary assessment outcomes. Working as a member of this committee afforded me new opportunities to gain leadership experience. During my time on this committee, we were asked to oversee the evaluation on one of the secondary outcomes—

Having the opportunity to lead, but also to pause and learn from my missteps, was paramount to my professional development.

information literacy. The last time the college assessed information literacy it used the Project Standardized Assessment of Information Literacy Skills (SAILS) as its assessment instrument. I was asked to lead this new process to evaluate the implementation of and integration of information literacy into the curriculum at GCC. One of my duties was to review other instruments and make a recommendation to the committee. After careful review of the available tools, my recommendation was to continue with Project SAILS. The committee agreed with my finding that using SAILS again would allow us to more effectively compare and contrast our analysis with the previous results.

At the start of the next semester, GCC's English faculty was informed of the upcoming assessment. Working with the college's institutional research office, a selected number of course sections were identified for inclusion in the assessment. The coordination and oversight of communicating with the selected English faculty and courses was definitely another leadership opportunity that involved many proctors, primarily library faculty. Doing all the necessary assessment, analysis, and report writing involved many separate time-consuming tasks, and at times it required me to constantly remind others to complete their assessment work. This experience provided me with a greater understanding of how I could lead.

Taking on additional college committee assignments expanded my leadership skills. I spent time working on faculty searches, budget, strategy, accreditation, and even district-wide library online resources. These areas of focus have enhanced my presentation, communication, and negotiating skills. No matter which issues came up in any of these committees, I approached them as opportunities to lead, whether formally or informally. To get the most out of committee work, do the necessary homework before you get to the meeting and be prepared to complete specific assignments on time. Being motivated to learn more about institutional issues and being ready to engage in discussions with colleagues positioned me to emerge as a leader among my fellow committee members. In my 11 years at GCC, opportunities have continued to expand my leadership knowledge and experience.

New Assignment

Looking back at what I have experienced at GCC, a vivid example of enlightening my knowledge and contribution became evident when in my third year at GCC, the library director asked me to become the head librarian for a new branch campus library. I appreciated his mentoring ever since my initial year with GCC. Before his asking me to take on this new role, we had lengthy discussions about my future and he always encouraged my pursuit of new learning opportunities, whether through professional development opportunities or a doctoral degree. The college had completed construction of new buildings for this branch campus, one of which was the library and computer center. Two college service units would be combined within this facility, the library and information technology. Additionally, this library would have only a small collection of print material, depending instead on electronic resources for its content. Another interesting feature would be the creation of a library commons area in the front part of the building. I saw all 17,000 square feet of this new facility as a leadership challenge. Working collaboratively with my information technology department colleagues would broaden my leadership perspective.

During the next six years, I experienced a plethora of unique issues as the head librarian for this facility. For example, there was one incident that involved a faculty and his class. Without any notice, they came into the library and computer center wanting a library orientation. Any librarian who has had this experience will understand exactly how I felt. As the evening librarian, I maintained my professionalism and delivered a general orientation of library services and resources. Later in the week, I had a discussion with the professor and shared a more appropriate way for him to schedule library orientation sessions. Leading a library that was considerably different from the one on the main campus, staying attuned to student needs for their assignments, and managing faculty expectations for this library became an ongoing educational opportunity. Providing the academic resources everyone needed in a somewhat nontraditional environment was a challenge to my leadership skills.

Life Happens

Being away from the main campus was invigorating and refreshing. Experimenting with different ways to provide library services via the Web was gratifying and occasionally disappointing. When services did not succeed or we experienced a failure, I found myself learning a great deal about how I might do things differently. If you initially fail, you begin to realize that it is possible to strategize and work toward a better solution that achieves the original goal. I enjoyed coleading this facility with my information technology colleague, but life intervened unexpectedly, as it often does. Regrettably, my mother was diagnosed with cancer. She lived in San Diego, California, and this presented a number of challenges and concerns as I regularly sought to attend to her medical care. After conferring with my Library Director, with support from Human Resources, I filed for intermittent FMLA (family medical leave) and was granted this type of leave. I was indeed fortunate to have supportive library colleagues who stepped in to help manage the day-to-day operations of our branch campus library while I was attending to my mother's health situation.

Deciding to Pursue the Doctorate

During fall 2007, my interest in pursuing an advanced degree was sparked again when I received an e-mail message distributed to all district employees. It came from the College of Education at Northern Arizona University, offering an invitation to an informational seminar regarding their educational leadership doctoral program. It was designed to create a special cohort of employees employed with the district who would have an opportunity to earn the education doctoral degree. After talking with my wife, my mother, and a few other colleagues, I came to the realization that I needed to pursue

This crucible moment provided me an opportunity to deeply reflect on my professional goals, and that was to become an academic library administrator. What did I learn from this moment in my life? Never give up on your goals.

this opportunity for several reasons. First, I am a first-generation Latino male and too few minorities have earned doctoral degrees, whether a Ph.D. or an Ed.D. If I were able to earn the degree, it would contribute to the diversification of the program. Second, while working at California State University, Long Beach and completing my master of public administration, I developed an appetite to continue on with my formal education in the leadership arena. Finally, I have always been fascinated with leadership and organizational culture. These two variables can lead an organization to success or failure. It just depends on the individuals and circumstances that exist within the leadership style that is being exercised.

If I desired to pursue a leadership career opportunity in the near future, especially within higher education, this degree would prepare me for such a possibility. I ultimately decided to apply to the Ed.D. program at Northern Arizona University and was admitted in summer 2008. Even with life's unexpected circumstances, I completed my program of study in 2012. My only regret with this new educational experience was the passing of my mother before I graduated. With her passing, I regained the energy and determination to complete my study and defend my dissertation later that fall. This educational experience transformed my thinking and daily living as a person, academic librarian, and leader.

In my first course, which had a community college focus, the professor influenced how I would begin to use my analytical skills in assessing leadership and community college issues. The main emphasis of his seminar was for his doctoral students to work in groups and research case studies from community college institutions. Each group would provide their recommendations to the class in seeking a solution. At the end of each presentation, our professor would summarize what actually took place at that institution. His pedagogical style left a lasting impression on me in beginning to comprehend the complexities in being a higher education leader. Fortunately, I would have other professors equally influential in my doctoral program. I consider myself quite lucky to have had these transformative experiences as an educational leadership doctoral student.

Leading Through Professional Associations

Beyond my formal education, I continued to stay active at the national level of the American Library Association. I have been an active member of this association ever since I was in library school. Once I graduated from my library science program and during my first few years of professional library work, I enrolled for membership in the Association of College & Research Libraries (ACRL). During my community college career I have been an active member of the Community Junior Colleges Libraries Section (CJCLS) of ACRL. After years of service on committees, I was elected by CJCLS members to be the vice-chair/chair/past chair of the section from 2012 to 2015. The combination of these opportunities has been rewarding since it gave me leadership experiences at the national level. When you are a member of an association, opportunities will arise for different types of leadership experiences. You may eventually lead a committee, section, or division, whether it is with the American Library Association or any other organization. Seize the moments that are presented in your career path.

I continue to be engaged with library associations but now I also serve in another nonlibrary higher education organization. I was recently appointed to the American Association of Community Colleges Commission on Research, Technology & Emerging Trends. This resulted in part from my leadership of CJCLS. When you least expect it, doors will begin to open that provide greater professional opportunities.

Leadership Roles in Governance

Not every librarian has faculty status, but for those who do there can be additional leadership opportunities in the institutional governance structure. I learned more about this when I was elected the college's faculty senate president. I was the first faculty librarian, as well as the first minority faculty member, to be elected to this post at my college. It was overwhelming and a proud moment to achieve something of historical significance. I began my duties as faculty senate president in April 2014. During the initial year, I have run the gamut of various shared governance experiences.

Within my first month as faculty senate president, a crisis arose regarding an academic department and the college administration. The argument between both parties dealt with an interpretation of the faculty policy manual. What I learned from this experience was to maintain my calm and gather the facts from both sides. Additionally, conferring with other faculty senate presidents within our district provided me with the appropriate level of information in providing a working solution to the academic department and administration in resolving their issue in a professional and productive way. Having this initial experience became a crucible in how I dealt with the situation and demonstrated my leadership to my colleagues. After one year, it had been an educational experience from many viewpoints.

My term concludes in April 2016. I will be mentoring the faculty senate president-elect prior to completing my term. Providing a relatively painless transition is one of my many remaining objectives as the current faculty leader. What I learned and experienced from my educational leadership program is reinforced by what I have learned and continue to experience as faculty senate president. It is important to remain professional and humble before making any final decision. In any circumstance, you rely on the experience of others to guide you in making a final decision.

My first year as faculty senate president was an accelerated year of experiences. Representing faculty and dialoguing with the college administration regarding various policy, budget, human resources, strategic, and accreditation issues was daunting and exhilarating. Literally, every day at work was different in many ways. Seeking information from colleagues, hearing out what had transpired, and consulting with the faculty senate kept me going, and at times made my days into nights. The end result is that I do not regret being elected faculty senate president because in only the first year, I gained a variety of experiences and discovered new skills. What I have learned during this period with these unexpected experiences has been quite valuable. I could not expect or anticipate acquiring this new knowledge from a leadership textbook. I remind myself that in order to deal with the unexpected,

I must remain fair, calm, collected, and decisive. I not only represent myself but also the college faculty.

What Have I Learned?

Remembering whom you represent is a reminder that will influence the type of leader you want to be. Relying on your foundation as a leader, being humble, fair, and inspirational, are elements that demonstrate your leadership acumen for any setting, whether at home or at work. In my 20-plus years as an academic librarian, I have experienced many types of leadership, but to grow as a leader, one must reflect on what was good or bad from each specific situation. Reflection is essential to improving your future leadership endeavors. Without taking leadership opportunities, whether they are formal or informal, I remind myself, what am I trying to do for the organization and myself? Knowing what your goal and objective is for pursuing leadership opportunities will provide you with a direction and energy to lead and inspire others. Understanding your strengths and weaknesses as a leader will further inform your leadership style and how you collaborate with other academic leaders when overseeing a project or organization. Leadership, from my perspective, is largely about human interaction. It is also about taking advantage of opportunities that arise and finding a path to leadership that works. There are times when we must deviate from the path we created in order to achieve the goal, which benefits the organization.

REFLECTIONS: KEY LESSONS FOR LEADERS

» Provide excellent contributions but go beyond your library work and be active in associations

» Reflect on your personal and professional life in order to enhance your future contributions

» Influence and encourage others to step up and contribute to the well-being of your organization

» Continue seeking formal and informal leadership opportunities in your professional and personal life

References

Alfred, Richard L. *Managing the Big Picture in Colleges and Universities: From Tactics to Strategy*. Westport, CT: Praeger, 2006.

Burns, James MacGregor. *Leadership*. New York: Harper & Row, 1978.

Gracia, Jorge J. E. *Hispanic/Latino Identity: A Philosophical Perspective*. Malden, MA: Wiley-Blackwell, 2000.

Kotter, John P. *Leading Change*. Cambridge, MA: Harvard Business School, 1996.

National Center for Supercomputing Applications at the University of Illinois. NCSA Mosaic. http://www.ncsa.illinois.edu/enabling/mosaic (Accessed July 2015).

Schein, Edgar H. *Humble Inquiry: The Gentle Art of Asking Instead of Telling*. San Francisco: Berrett-Koehler Publishers, 2013.

Schein, Edgar H. *Organizational Culture and Leadership*, 4th ed. San Francisco: Jossey-Bass, 2010.

Trueba, Enrique T. *Latinos Unidos: From Cultural Diversity to the Politics of Solidarity*. Lanham, MD: Rowman & Littlefield, 1999.

—— 10 ——

THE MINDFUL LEADER: FROM ACCIDENTAL TO INTENTIONAL LEADERSHIP

Kenley Neufeld

///////////// **TOP TAKEAWAYS IN THIS CHAPTER**

» Motivation and confidence are fundamentals for learning to be a leader

» Regular mindfulness practice cultivates improvement

» Knowledge building continues throughout your career

The adage "when the student is ready the teacher will appear" seems apropos to my career as I've learned the skills, received the training, and had the willingness to try something new when an opportunity has presented itself. Not without hard work, mind you. It has been an extraordinary journey and I found the support of my colleagues, my mentors, and my employers humbling time and time again. There have been many mistakes along the way and each has served as an opportunity to learn and do things differently the next time.

In my 20 years as a library professional, I have been an electronic media coordinator, a library and technology director, a reference librarian, an instructor, a technology librarian, a library director, and now a dean responsible for many areas outside the library. I've served in many leadership roles beyond the library such as president of local, regional, and statewide library organizations, as an academic senate president for a college faculty, and as a teacher and mentor for an international Buddhist organization. On some level, I did pursue each role but each was pursued when conditions arose and presented themselves. At each step along the way, I was motivated to fill a need—either personally or for the organization.

Roots of Leadership

In Spring 1993, I was 25 years old and enrolled in my first semester of library school at San Jose State University. I was living in San Francisco, an hour drive from San Jose, and enrolled in two classes that incorporated online material as part of the curriculum—Reference and Information Services and Microcomputers in Libraries. I had only recently bought my first computer and wanted to access the class materials remotely without having to travel to San Jose all the time. So down the rabbit hole of Windows 3.1, screeching dial-up modems, and text-based terminal windows I went, in order to gain connection to this new world of online information. In addition to my library courses, I spent countless hours cramming my head full of information about this "new" thing called the Internet. I was obsessed with learning. I was motivated to teach myself. And I was having fun doing it. As that first semester drew to a close, the beta version of Mosaic was released and the world was forever changed. The graphical Web was born and this became not only a crucible moment for the world but served as a catalyst that framed the next decade of my career.

First a Technology Leader

Though I didn't set out to be a leader, the conditions that allowed my leadership to grow and blossom can be traced back to my graduate school years where I learned confidence, motivation, willingness, experimenting, trying new things, and having fun while doing it. Many years later, I realized that my experiences in graduate school were the beginning of my library leadership. I had an internal motivation, along with a confidence that a task could be accomplished. There is a certain amount of acting "as if" to help push us forward that can motivate us, inspire us to ask questions, and embrace the unknown. The foundation of motivation and confidence is to have the willingness to learn. My personal learning forced me to look beyond what was available or taught in the library school. A certain level of obsession complemented my internal motivation and confidence. There were many nights when I spent hours and hours reading documentation, experimenting with outcomes, and making mistakes before a breakthrough arrived. It was at graduate school that a technologist was born.

The conditions for becoming a technologist were purely accidental. I was in the right place (Silicon Valley), at the right time (1993), studying the right topic (library science). In those days one didn't need specific training or certifications to be considered an expert on the Internet. Learn a little HTML, create a Web page, and you were golden. When I enrolled in library school, I wasn't thinking about being a technology leader or a library leader—I wanted to be a librarian because I liked working in libraries.

There is a certain amount of acting 'as if' to help push us forward which can motivate us, inspire us to ask questions and embrace the unknown. The foundation of motivation and confidence is to have the willingness to learn.

I liked learning. I was pulled into the technology serendipitously by being in the Bay Area at the advent of the Internet. This in turn pushed me into the leadership roles that provided my first opportunities to lead programs and services in the area of technology. Beyond the basic nuts and bolts of management I was unprepared for the responsibilities of true leadership. I quickly learned it requires people skills that go beyond intellectual knowledge.

Being a library technology leader in the 1990s was a unique place to be professionally. Though technology had been a key part of libraries and library work for decades, the arrival of the graphical Internet followed by Windows 95 both radically transformed how people interacted with information. My first librarian position was not a formal leadership position and yet, because it dealt almost exclusively with technology, others looked to me for leadership and guidance. What should we be teaching students? What types of technologies should we bring into the library and into the classroom? There were a lot of unknowns in those days and the media wrote frequently about technology and the "Wild West" of the Internet. The World Wide Web, as we called it in those days, had everyone's interest yet very few people at my small academic institution knew much about it. This unknown placed me in a position of experience and leadership as others sought to understand this period of technical transformation. Within the academy, I offered computer and Internet courses, established network access to CD-ROM towers of library databases, and built a library Web site. Within our regional professional network of primary and secondary school librarians, I was pushed forward to help every-one better understand this new digital landscape.

Time for Change

Being a leader in my first library position can be partially attributed to being at the right place at the right time. I was working as a librarian in a very small setting—an exclusive Bay Area private school with only 400 students. I was young, had the time to commit to continued learning, and was passionate about the work. There was room to learn, to experiment, and to be recognized. I wasn't hired into a leadership role but my seeming luck, my natural passion for learning new material and technologies, and my willingness to share that knowledge gave me the reputation of an innovator on campus. I was willing to take risks where others were not. My ideas were met with both enthusiasm and resistance.

Three years later, an opportunity to push myself further presented itself at another private school in the region—the position of Library Director at a larger private school. I pursued the opportunity with gusto and found myself with a beautiful library, a computer lab, a staff, a budget, and title that brought with it leadership expectations. Many secondary schools at the time were uncertain about the huge impact technology was having on learning and needed guidance on how to fund projects and services and professional skills to meet this growing need. I pitched an idea to the school during my interview for the Library Director position to include the Technology Director role. That led the institution to create a new position of Library and Technology Director that served the entire campus. They had a demonstrated need for a technology-savvy librarian, I had the skills, and the school was willing to negotiate and experiment with something innovative. The high school included one other librarian and a computer teacher who had been responsible for the campus technology. These two were enthusiastic—partially because they didn't need to be in charge anymore—to have someone new enter the campus and provide the technology and library leadership.

The next four years were extremely rewarding and challenging. I made more mistakes in this role than in any other position since because I still didn't have the people skills to manage people and to effectively communicate change. Two specific aspects of this role were particularly challenging. First, I was at least two decades younger than the other two employees in my area. They had a wealth of knowledge and experience, but not in the areas that I was pushing the institution to move. Second, the technology was moving so fast that it brought an overwhelming feeling to the staff. As a young man, I had yet to learn how to communicate effectively and to have patience in initiating change. The first year was a struggle but as we moved into the second year, greater trust and friendship had developed that allowed change to occur more easily. I too had learned to observe other library leaders to see how they led their organizations and supported their employees. It was truly a sandbox for my leadership skills.

The long hours continued, the learning continued, and the expectations increased. I was 30 years old and didn't know how to work well with the diversity of a larger organization. I had to work within an organization where most people were considerably older than I was and they had been doing the same work for decades. I was called upon to implement new systems—digital library services, upgraded networking, new e-mail communications, and database resources for the campus—that caused anxiety for the employees. The employees just wanted things to work without any disruption to their workflow and my job often revolved around training and reassuring people. Working with the technology was definitely challenging, and I knew how to learn in that area, but the technology challenges were easy compared to learning to work with my colleagues. I still hadn't learned patience, understanding, and an awareness of working well with people. Despite this challenge, I was able to propel the institution forward by providing integrated library and technology support and services. We were a demonstrated leader in our region for experimenting with and implementing technology and library services. The regional library network elected me leader of the organization. Everything in the mainstream media was enamored with the "dot com bubble" and the library literature was focused on the impact the Internet was having on libraries and library services.

I had sought out this leadership role but I didn't always feel prepared to take on the responsibility. It was during this time that my learning needed to switch from a technology focus to a focus on people and learning about leadership, management, and working well with others. Awareness of my weaknesses as a colleague, a communicator, and a leader became very clear to me during this time. How do I communicate complex change to an entrenched employee? How do I empower others with skills to solve problems? How do I manage employees who report to me when I don't have any experience being a supervisor? I needed to learn these skills and learn them fast. I think being a leader means being aware of our own weaknesses and then being able to find ways to improve, learn, and grow. This awareness continues to frame my development as a leader 20 years later. Just like the technology change that was all around me, there needed to be a personality change in this young library professional.

Gaining New Skills and Perspectives

Being in a small library, and within an organization that didn't have a formal leadership program, forced me to look beyond my own organization to cultivate leadership skills. The regional library network had senior library leaders who were seasoned in the areas of management and people skills. I sought out relationships with these role models at various times. Seeking out this kind of learning doesn't always mean formal mentoring because so much can be learned from just asking a question at the right time. More important, learning to thoughtfully observe behavior helps you evolve into your own great teacher of leadership. How do those I admire hold themselves? When do they choose to say something and when do they choose to remain silent? How do others react to them? Learning to emulate the successful behavior of other skilled leaders can be transformative if it can be successfully applied. On the more formal side, I took coursework on workplace communication, was selected for the American Library Association's 1997 Emerging Leader program, began graduate studies on conflict management and mediation, and started a daily meditation practice.

My motivation to become a better worker, a better colleague, and a better leader was very strong. Making this effort while continuing to serve as the Library and Technology Director supported my growing leadership skill set. The qualities I needed to learn may come naturally to those born leaders about whom we may hear. My experience was quite different. It taught me that leadership, like any desired skill, requires fine-tuning and cultivation in order to fully develop. Through personal reflections, keen observations, and formal training for specific skills, I became a better leader. And despite all that, after seven years of working closely with technology, providing leadership and innovation, and becoming known as a library leader, I was ready to recede into the background and take a break.

Mindfulness in Leadership

Sharing my leadership experience and success requires a discussion of mindfulness practice. During the following four years I continued to work as a librarian at a community college, and the focus of my life shifted more internally and away from library leadership. My wife and I had relocated to my hometown and we were busy raising our two young children. My job was blocks from home so I was able to bike to work and be home for lunch on most days to see my family. Not being in a formal leadership role for those four years was a blessing as it provided the space for me to gain better insight and understanding into myself. But the crucible for me at that time, and another accidental moment on my path, was the 9/11 terrorist attacks. This world event shook me to my core and forced me to ask myself if I was doing enough for myself, my community, and for the well-being of the world. And so, after several years of experimenting and practicing with daily meditation in the late 1990s, it was during this period that my mindfulness practice became more central to my life because I saw it as a vehicle to make a positive change in the world. These years helped me mature and deepen both personally and professionally. They also contributed to my continued training as a leader.

Mindfulness was not a technique I pursued to build leadership skills but a practice from which it sprang. Putting more time and energy into my mindfulness and meditation practice helped me become a better leader. Mindfulness is the energy of being aware and awake to the present moment. It is the continuous practice of touching life deeply in every moment of daily life. To be mindful is to be truly alive, present and at one with those around you and with what you are doing. We bring our body and mind into harmony

I had sought out this leadership role but I didn't always feel prepared to take on the responsibility. It was during this time that my learning needed to switch from a technology focus to a focus on people and learning about leadership, management, and working well with others.

while we wash the dishes, drive the car, talk to a colleague, or take our morning shower. Though mindfulness practice is intended to be continuous throughout the day, we can also spend focused time practicing in the form of intentional sitting meditation or walking meditation. Setting aside time each day to just be quiet and present for our body and mind is key. Breathing in and breathing out, bringing our full attention to the action of the breath. It's that simple. And through this practice, one may gain some personal insight and personal understanding. This then provides the framework to be clear, calm, and creative because it helps minimize the internal dialogue, the doubts, and the fears that are a part of the human condition.

I believe this idea of mindfulness practice is central to my future leadership success. Mindfulness practice helps us to understand our mind and offers spaciousness to our thinking. We can train ourselves to have stillness and quiet, and from that place of clarity we are able to discover and take the right action. One practical method of using mindfulness practice is when I am grappling with something difficult. For example, there have been times when a strained and uncomfortable professional relationship exists with an employee. This needs my attention, primarily because it is someone I will need to continue interacting with daily. With mindfulness, I can set time to quiet my mind, quiet my body, and then investigate the relationship from a place of calm in order to identify the next action. It could be as simple as seeing the person as a person with needs, desires, and suffering and all I need to do as a manager is have more compassion. This awareness can arise from the stillness.

In my work environment, walking meditation is very practical. Because the academic environment is typically comprised of a campus of buildings and open space, there is always the opportunity to take a walk during the course of a workday—even if it's a mindful walk to your next class or meeting. I've discovered that I'm at my best as a leader when I take time away from the office, away from the computer, and away from meetings. Setting a timer on the computer as a reminder to take a break is an effective method to remind us to take care of ourselves. Step outside and allow yourself to be fully present for a walk with nowhere to go and nothing to do. If you don't have the time for a walking break, then use the time when moving between buildings for a meeting. Set aside your worries, set aside your cell phone, and allow your mind to relax by bringing your attention to each footstep and aligning it with your breathing. You will arrive at your meeting fresh and relaxed.

Up until this point, my professional development and meditation practice had been mostly self-taught and self-motivated. Part of what happened on 9/11 was that it clarified for me that our personal and professional journeys are not separate. We need each area of our lives to fuel the other. I was able to incorporate mindfulness into my work and personal life thanks to good spiritual friends. These friends became my mentors and inspiration for continued learning and growing as a person and as a leader. Within the spiritual community, I began to stretch my leadership wings again and rediscovered that I truly enjoyed being a leader. From this I learned that mentorship is critical to my well-being and for the well-being of those around me. From this time forward, I have actively sought out and maintained mentor relationships, both professionally and spiritually, to continue learning and growing.

An Investment in Leadership

In 2005, I applied for and was offered the position of Technology Librarian at Santa Barbara City College (SBCC). I held this position for one year before I was promoted to Library Director. Though I had aspirations for library administration, I did not seek the director position nor did I apply for the director position—the college leadership identified me and invited me to take on the role and responsibility. Though unusual, I had my suspicion the college was interviewing me for the Library Director position from the start because they offered me the new role within months of starting at the institution. It was an uncomfortable year as the outgoing Library Director remained and yet the library staff knew that I was going to be the new director. The senior management was seeking a change agent for the library and identified me as a person willing to experiment with change. In many ways, it came down to willingness, ability, and attitude. I wanted to do the very best I could in this new position, and yet memories of my last director position still lingered, causing uncertainty and fear to arise. Therefore, after one year in the position, I invested in the ACRL/Harvard Leadership Institute to guide me on my way to becoming a leader.

The training I received at Harvard, combined with my mindfulness practice, better prepared me to lead. I gained insight into knowing myself and it also greatly improved my communication skills. In particular, the communication skill in which I've most improved is listening. One of the foundational trainings in mindfulness practice is learning how to listen, really listen, and learning when not to speak. As a library leader, I needed to be able to listen to my staff and listen to the students. I needed to be able to offer them my full attention. I designed the conditions in my work environment to facilitate better listening. What kind of environment am I creating for the students and staff who visit my office? I've found that a clean and organized office space goes a long way for setting my mind at ease and the mind of my visitor. I have a few pieces of art with affirmations to remind me to be present. The desktop space between the guest and myself is clear and free from distraction and my computer is set up so it's not visible to me while talking with a guest.

Over a period of several years, I found myself with increasing responsibilities that extended well beyond the library walls. This in turn supported the library and gave voice to the library and its needs across the campus. We were viewed as innovative leaders in customer service, technology, and outreach. Our outreach and presence beyond the library brought more students to the library and increased the number of classes we taught. The transformation of the library at SBCC was dramatic as we doubled both our collection budget and the number of students using the library within my first three years as library director. In addition to being the Library Director, I was elected president of the Academic Senate—the body representing all 650 faculty members at the college to the administration and the board of trustees.

I quickly learned that being an effective leader at SBCC meant being willing to experiment and being comfortable with making mistakes. I had confidence and I had willingness—two additional characteristics of an effective leader. My vision for the library was to create a central gathering place for students to explore, to learn, and to grow. This meant creating a welcoming environment and then doing intentional outreach to the students and the faculty. The library staff was hungry for change and to be empowered, and this made the first year easy. Together, we focused on making the library a welcoming and engaging place to visit, and the staff was ready for this change. Naturally, we became inundated with students and requests for programming and services.

A few years later, I introduced the idea of replacing our legacy library catalog system. Our move to a new library system took all of my leadership capital of the preceding years. The staff knew change, they knew we were recognized as library leaders, trust had been established, and yet this brought about a great deal of fear. Changing a library system is significant, but changing to a newly developed system installed in very few libraries caused even more anxiety. Through team meetings, product demonstrations, and directing staff to take key leadership responsibilities, I made the decision to move to the new system. We were not 100 percent in agreement to move forward but there was consensus to proceed and the staff did their best to implement and embrace the new system. This change was a challenge to my leadership and our organization emerged successfully from this test to our cohesiveness because of the trust we had built over the years and because of my confidence and willingness to push a new product.

Confidence comes from experience and one of the ways to gain that experience is through knowledge building. The more we know and understand our organization and our work culture, the better leaders we will become. A certain level of obsession about knowing the college is critical—its culture, programs, services, policies, and people. Knowing how to navigate the system and understanding how the system functions, even in areas not directly relevant, can provide a foundation of knowledge to serve both the department and the broader organization. This requires listening to others, asking lots of questions, taking the time to read documentation, and getting engaged in as

Mindfulness was not a technique I pursued to build leadership skills but a practice from which it sprang. Putting more time and energy into my mindfulness and meditation practice helped me become a better leader.

many areas as possible that support the library and our role on campus. For example, most academic institutions are rife with committees. For me, this knowledge-building period included actively engaging with several committees. The benefit was twofold: first, I learned more about the operations of the institution as a whole, and second, I was able to embody the library to faculty and staff beyond the library itself.

Leading for Change

Confidence carries with it responsibility as we learn to speak up, advocate, and inform decisions for the library and for the organization. On the flip side, willingness serves a leader in two ways. We need a willingness to learn and understand our libraries, our organizations, and ourselves, but having willingness is also having the ability to say "yes." As a leader, I have learned to say "yes" when there is a need for the library or for the organization. I work hard and people observe this strength in me, and this in turn brings more responsibility. But saying "yes" as a leader also means saying "yes" to the team with their ideas, their visions, and their innovations. Empowering the staff to experiment and be risky pushes the individual, the institution, and me as a leader. I have learned to empower those around me to get things done in a way that is meaningful to them.

Library leadership calls for knowledge building, mindfulness, strong communication skills, confidence, and willingness. Another aspect of library leadership I have eluded to is experimentation. By experimentation I mean testing out ideas and concepts in a real-life setting—just going for it! Staff members bring great ideas to the table but are often not empowered to implement those ideas. It is important to cultivate an environment where new ideas are encouraged and given the go-ahead. However, it must be clear that if the experiment doesn't succeed, it's important to revisit the effort through a new lens, applying the learning you received from mistakes and failures. Don't be afraid to leave some ideas behind. Sometimes an experiment is a flop. We tend to think that because we've invested time and energy into a project or idea we cannot abandon it. A good leader knows when to continue to pursue a project and when to let go. It is also important that library leaders bring their ideas to the table and work with the staff to implement and try out those ideas. Leaders can push and be bold but it is equally important to be communicative and not get attached to outcomes. When something isn't working, then stop doing it.

Change can be difficult and resistance is always going to exist, but this shouldn't be a barrier to proceeding. As a library leader, it is your responsibility to move things forward even if lacking complete buy-in on a project. For example, moving from an antiquated library automation system may be necessary but it will also push everyone to learn new systems and processes. Not everyone is going to want that experience, even if it is the right thing for the user community. Our library moved from a decade-old library system to a cutting-edge system that was completely different. The time was ripe. The choice was clear. We made the switch and most of the staff was accepting, but for others it was a challenge. Establishing a method for communication and training was necessary to make this transition successful. Being willing to change processes, even more than once, was a part of this adoption.

I served as Library Director at Santa Barbara City College for eight years. It was a transformative period both for the library and for myself professionally. Both the library and I received awards and accolades both locally and nationally. Over 50 percent of the library staff retired during these years and I had the fortunate experience of building a team of passionate and dedicated professionals interested in doing their very best for the library and our students. I served as chair for over a dozen campus-wide committees and was ultimately elected president of the Academic Senate. Our statewide organization, the Council of Chief Librarians, elected me president, and this allowed me to have significant interaction with the Chancellor's Office and other statewide leadership groups. This unfolding of events is all due to hard work, kind mentors, knowledge building, a great willingness, experimentation, and confidence in my abilities. These opportunities would not have been successful without the support and diligent efforts of the library staff. My leadership path took a lot of effort and responsibility, but in other ways it was a natural unfolding of everything that came before, combined with my willingness to say "yes."

In July 2014, I transitioned to a "non-library" administrative position as a dean. For the first time in 20 years, I don't walk into a library every morning.

My responsibilities have expanded significantly into the broader academy as I serve as dean for the library and the departments of English as Second Language, School of Modern Languages, and Physical Education and Health. My other leadership responsibilities include faculty professional development, student learning outcomes, and all aspects of the large distance education program at Santa Barbara City College. My foundation of 20 years in the library, along with the leadership skills I developed along the way, established this opportunity for me to move outside the library. Taking on this new role was very intentional and not accidental in any way. The change is significant and represents a new crucible moment in my career. In just a short time, there have already been new challenges and unexpected surprises that demonstrate there will be more crucible moments to come. The library remains part of my professional world and I am actively mentoring the new Library Director and remain engaged with library leadership in the state.

REFLECTIONS: KEY LESSONS FOR LEADERS

» Cultivating compassion and understanding of ourselves, and for those with whom we work, will transform our work environments along with the programs and services that we offer

» Cultivating patience and calm has allowed those who look to me for leadership to have greater confidence and to know they are supported

» Leaders should be able to pivot—whether on a small project or on a career change—with confidence

$$\text{————}\ 11\ \text{————}$$

VOICE ACTIVATION PROTOCOL

Char Booth

///////// TOP TAKEAWAYS IN THIS CHAPTER

» It is essential to examine what it means to self-identify as a leader

» A critical step toward realizing the combination of personal and professional empowerment that leadership entails is to identify and confront factors that may lead you to suppress, question, and/or mishear your own voice

» Conviction, vision, support, and elasticity are qualities that facilitate principled and productive professional action

Since the outset of my career, encountering the term *leadership* has caused a series of visceral reactions. In the beginning, I experienced a mingled sense of confusion, hesitation, and conflict. Confusion about what leadership meant to those who invoked it: leading whom, and to where exactly? Was this some universal series of traits and actions that only the clued-in understood, which apparently did not include myself? Hesitation in the sense that I should be *doing* leadership but had no idea how, having just begun to work in an organizational world that I had little insight into and less than stellar confidence in my abilities. Conflict in the form of how to act ethically and with conviction while working with a familiar ambition to excel and be recognized, ambition that I can only assume was burned into my psyche by a particular form of upper-middle-class grooming predicated on reaching the mirage of *professional success.*

My reactions to leadership have morphed over time—fast-forward a few years and the notion has become less obscure. For my own part, pride in hard work and cultivating a strong sense of conviction have helped clarify and depressurize a positive notion of leadership in the abstract. Adjusting to the reality of decisive action in a series of "increasingly responsible" positions has lessened my hesitation. Insight into and engagement with the profession and its larger discourse have revealed a leadership formula of sorts, one with established channels of participation that facilitate the requisite and oft-invoked act of "stepping up." Observation of those achieving leadership status of varying degrees has revealed certain positive characteristics implied by the term, as well as their antitheses (which can as easily manifest as the positives, particularly in the self-conscious act of leading).

All of that said, an underlying conflict remains when the discussion of leadership becomes more concrete: what it means to self-identify as a *leader*, and whether the implications of such an identification are actually desirable. Even when motivated by excellent intentions and vision, I believe that individuals who are compelled to lead operate under a conditioned ambition to achieve; and it is critical for those of us who possess this trait to examine how to best channel it toward meaningful and reflective action. The urgency in this examination is based on the simple fact that leadership and success are inextricably linked in the vernacular. Leadership and authority are similarly (and problematically) linked. To misinterpret leadership as success and/or authority is to be driven by a self-centered ambition that substitutes the good of one's resume and/or ego for a larger good. To crave recognition as a leader without a balance of purpose, humility, and care for others can become an addiction in which the experience of this external feedback is an end in itself.

To crave recognition as a leader without a balance of purpose, humility, and care for others can become an addiction in which the experience of this external feedback is an end in itself.

Leadership without heart and embodiment is a form of professional sociopathy, the results of which are transient at their best and at their worst can harm others. Expressed in the working world, this is when "leaders" become heartless and disembodied, and perpetuate a series of imbalanced paradigms that dominate society. Which is to say that one can attain *positions* of leadership through behavior that can be described as anything but, and that all of us are helped and/or hindered by well-documented sociological and cultural factors at work under the surface of human interactions—the very real *"isms"* that impede and facilitate life trajectories on a daily basis. One need only look to the gender, class, and racial composition of the executive level of basically anything for evidence of this fact. My own career path has been formed by a desire to challenge as many of these "isms" as possible, a compelling reason as any I can identify to "lead": to represent and advocate for difference where decisions are made in order to initiate meaningful change.

To contribute to this volume implies to some extent that I think of myself as a leader, which is a somewhat distasteful prospect and not precisely accurate—not so much from a sense of reluctance or disdain for the idea of leadership per se but from an impetus to question such labels and their implications. At the same time, it presents a significant opportunity to articulate certain insights to those with an ostensible motivation to make an impact of one sort or another. This task has required me to embark on a process of examination: why do I possess a vague distaste for the idea of leadership, while at the same time an appreciation of the importance of embodying certain personal and professional characteristics that result in good? The appreciation comes from observing those who work well and improve things for their organizations, stakeholders, and colleagues, and a consequent desire to emulate and affirm their work. The distaste seems to be grounded in antipathy for some of the problematic social constructs and human characteristics associated with leadership vying with an internalized sense of imposter syndrome—a powerful and culturally cultivated self-silencer manifesting in a fight/flight response to working scenarios that involve significant personal risk or extension. Thus comes the crux or "crucible" of this chapter. Many who could represent difference in leadership and most effectively confront its *isms*—the very people most needed to inform and direct decisions in all areas of endeavor—face great external and internal challenges to engagement, not only in terms of opportunity and access, but with the very notion of being leaders. Whether and how these challenges can be isolated and allayed is where I hope to make my contribution to this discussion.

Fear and Fearlessness

I believe that a fundamental leadership behavior is fearlessness. Yet, for the female-identified and those allied with communities of difference (for example, the individuals most touched by the oppression of *isms*), fear can be a constant aspect of life. This fear takes many forms: physical, emotional, economic, and so forth. Fear of failure, fear of rejection, fear of persecution, fear of retribution, fear of injustice. These fears can be conscious or unconscious, pervasive or subtle, but they are always destructive and sometimes incapacitating. Beyond the stacked external deck of privilege and oppression, internal fears can result in trepidation and uncertainty; these are decidedly *not* leadership behaviors. If it is necessary to surmount fear in order to make contributions that matter on a larger scale, then isolating strategies for understanding and confronting internal obstacles are essential. Particularly for those from "nontraditional" backgrounds and experiences: more than ever, the status quo establishment (writ small and large) needs us to help change its game.

Now for a fear self-analysis. As a white person raised in an upper-middle-class background by supportive, educated, and financially solvent parents, I am the recipient of a tremendous amount of social and economic privilege. That I expressed a nonconforming gender and sexual orientation at a young age in a conservative Texas town meant that I was also the recipient of traumatic experiences of violence and persecution. Paradoxically, this created as many catalysts to self-possession as it did impediments—as I was reviled I began to perceive the causes and conditions that produced hostility and, further, injustice for what it was and justice for what it should be. I developed a sense of defiance through the daily antagonisms and was compelled to learn how to confront prejudice directly and defend myself when necessary. Through this lived experience of intolerance I forged a strong identity, and in being outcast I learned to focus on principle, survival, and what came *next*.

As much as I learned to look beyond the present situation and react with power to antagonism, I also developed a habit of keeping my head down in order to not draw attention. I did what many who endure social rejection do: I receded in order to avoid instigation and formed a habit of not speaking up unless challenged. Combine this with the aforementioned imposter syndrome and I had years of disinclination toward engagement to undo as I began my career.

A significant challenge to any individual who would seek to embody positive, advocacy-based leadership is to suppress, question, and/or mishear their own voice. Many of us, particularly the female-identified, gender non-conforming, and/or members of various communities of difference, suffer from forms of self-doubt and subtle silencing. Gender, culture, orientation, and class can all exacerbate the internal or external suppression of voice, but self-questioning and indecision are near-universal experiences in working life. I speak from knowledge that these tendencies inhibit two crucial elements of the amalgamation of characteristics that "leadership" represents: principled and skillful communication of conviction through experience, and confidence that it will *matter*. Those who lead effectively have developed strategies for challenging their own hesitations and barriers, strategies that simultaneously make them more aware of and equipped to alleviate the trials that others experience. I can identify a series of factors that have helped me stop suppressing, questioning, and/or mishearing my own voice, a critical step toward realizing the combination of personal and professional empowerment that represents my own perception of what it means to lead:

Conviction. Vision. Support. Elasticity.

These factors have compelled me to build faith in my capacity to influence my organization and its stakeholders as well as libraries on a larger scale to the greater good. I believe that self-doubt can be transformed into thoughtfulness by substituting insight for insecurity, and this conscious action is essential for anyone who seeks to lead. For the remainder of this chapter, I will offer perspectives on my experiences of the above qualities in order to suggest a heuristic for pursuing the positive, care-focused, courageous, and, most importantly, voice-activated orientation to work that I believe "leadership" represents.

Conviction

Why do you do what you do? Are you driven by a belief in the value of your work, and can you articulate what led you to it? I have observed that librarians

A significant challenge to any individual who would seek to embody positive, advocacy-based leadership is to suppress, question, and/or mishear their own voice.

and other library types tend to be drawn to the field—called, if you will—which is an enormous advantage to cultivating a compelling professional voice. It is far easier to advocate for a purpose and advocacy is at the root of making a significant mark on any project, organization, or profession. In my own case, I was raised by educator parents to have a love for literacy and libraries, and I attended an undergraduate college (Reed) that orbits around a fabulously inclusive library. Students basically lived there, we (thought we) owned the place, and it helped us excel as learners and in community. By the time I completed my undergraduate degree, although I hadn't yet decided to pursue a career in libraries, I knew they would always play a prominent role in my life. Once I recognized that I wanted to help libraries maintain prominence in others' lives, the choice of a next step was clear.

It is incumbent upon leaders to hold convictions about the purpose of the work that they do, to be guided by touchstones that provide the philosophical foundation for practical action. Libraries are complex organisms and the values they represent are deeply held by those allied with them, but not necessarily by others: it is incumbent upon us to connect the latter to the contributions we make, a connection that is much better facilitated by personal conviction than mere statistics or stating (what we believe to be) the obvious. By identifying and cultivating our convictions, the work becomes about something larger than whether we as individuals succeed or fail, thus creating a more inclusive vision—this has been extremely helpful to me in overcoming my own trepidations about speaking up and out.

In order to communicate convictions effectively, it is necessary to thread your experiences into a personal/professional narrative that can provide motivation and inform the process of advocacy. This narrative can help to isolate areas of specialization that can be best informed by your efforts, and follow you throughout your career as it is shaped by the experiences and values you accumulate. For example: In graduate school I volunteered for a books-to-prisoners organization in Austin, Texas (Inside Books). This showed me that for many of the incarcerated, the dog-eared paperbacks we sent via mail was the only way to connect to reading/learning material, thanks in large part to dwindling prison library facilities. This experience began to challenge my rarified idea of libraries and their purpose among the disenfranchised, and to crystallize what remains my guiding principle in work: that access to information is a right, and it takes constant reaffirmation of that fact by those dedicated to making sure it does not devolve into a privilege. Watching for examples of information underprivilege and those social constructs that perpetuate them has led me to a belief in critical pedagogy, open access, and the responsibility of those with access to support those without—all of which have resulted in fascinating projects and collaborations of which I am proud. I believe deeply in this value, and am thus better equipped to articulate it in a way that different audiences can connect to.

Re: Conviction, ask yourself: How did I end up in this field, and is it where I belong? How do my experiences complicate and enrich the work that I do? How can I compellingly articulate my trajectory to someone who asks, *"why libraries?"* Do I have a guiding conviction informed by experience, and what does the life I've lived help me bring to my profession? If I hesitate in communicating my conviction, what might I do to cultivate greater confidence?

Vision

Cultivating a clear and achievable vision is one of the most important tasks for anyone who seeks to motivate others and/or themselves to get things done, particularly things of significance. Vision, as it is often discussed in relation to work, spans a broad spectrum, from projects and personal trajectories to organizational futures. One commonality of visions of all kinds is that they often begin as an intangible, a felt or expressed sense of what is possible but not yet realized. A compellingly articulated and thoroughly explored vision can provide a strong foundation for concrete and executable plans. However, vision that is vague and implemented without adequate structure, buy-in, or sensitivity to the extent of its impact can wreak havoc on organizations and initiatives, leading to justified confusion and alienation among the very people most needed to help achieve it.

My jobs have always had an element of creating new services, tools, structures, departments, and/or roles. I have learned the hard way that when a vision for any of these things is one-dimensional—that is, when created in isolation without appropriate consultation—it has a significant likelihood of failing to be embraced or understood. In organizational contexts, things like "vision statements" can be produced seemingly from thin air, coming off as more of a directive than a communal purpose. Being asked to toe the line to a new way of doing things that you did not have a say in or at least insight into its development is not inspiring—it is authoritarian. Vision is necessarily consultative and, if pursued strategically in community, can be the ultimate exercise in exercising one's voice in concert with others. This takes a great deal of self-questioning and dialogue, which, although it can feel like spinning wheels, is actually a process of education and consensus building that helps people feel heard and represented.

Vision applies to more than projects and institutions, of course—vision guides individuals to act and react, to direct themselves toward aims of what they want to be and do that may extend far into the future. I have known some people with a remarkably lucid picture of their career trajectory: where it is headed (even down to the institution) and what it will require to get there, almost like a series of steps on a ladder. While this is absolutely valid and enviably distinct, I have never approached my career with this degree of certainty. I have been hired into positions that seemed interesting in organizations I respected, and, while I have always had ideas of what I hoped to achieve in these roles, I have not been guided by a specific end goal. I have found that if I have a personal vision for work, it is to contribute to the culture of an institution in a way that enriches, alongside colleagues that I respect and enjoy working with. The moments in my career in which I became motivated by a more relentless version of what and where I wanted to be were easily the most conflicted, and when my voice began to feel as though it belonged to someone else. While my output may have been intense, it began to lack the connection and sustainability that I now understand is the most important guiding picture I can hold.

If vision is the ability to imagine what could and should be, how does one cultivate a capacity for not only *seeing* ahead to a different future or outcome but identifying the resources to actualize it? What makes for an achievable vision in any of these contexts? There is no simple answer, but truly knowing the situation you are in, seeing its weak and strong points, understanding its stakeholders (including yourself), and determining with careful consideration what is needed to affect change are all key.

Re: Vision, ask yourself: Have I formed a clear picture of what can be, and have I considered what it will take to get there? If those resources are not fully available, can this vision be adjusted to reality? Am I capable of integrating the ideas of others into this vision in the form of compromise, and have I done everything I can to mobilize and empower collaborators to share their perspectives? If my vision and principles are not in sync with my current position, am I ready to consider if a move in a different direction is preferable and/or feasible?

Support

I have had the pleasure of managing a number of highly creative and productive employees over the course of my career. I have also been engaged in difficult personnel scenarios related to employees facing significant personal and professional challenges that adversely affected their work and/or the broader organization. Over the course of this process I have learned the important lesson that none of these individuals were any more or less deserving of support—indeed, the more disaffected had usually been conditioned by a lack of consideration by those in leadership roles who did not perceive them as instrumentally deserving of attention.

I have been mentored throughout my life, at low moments and at high, and have been lucky to have been shown the combination of personal care and contextual sensitivity that excellent mentorship entails. When this came in times of greatest uncertainty and difficulty, it was the most effective by far: in this sense, true mentors see not only the potential of promising individuals but the humanity of all they encounter.

For example: I had a few teachers in high school who realized that the best way to help me was to allow me to *not* be there when my situation was at its most challenging. Absenteeism was obviously frowned upon by the authorities, but it was clear that the act of being present was what was preventing me from succeeding (or perhaps surviving?) at that time in my life. I had shown that I would do the work, gratefully, when allowed to escape from antipathetic educational surroundings—thus began a conspiracy of mutually consensual absence that helped me not only to graduate early and get out of a very trying circumstance but also to cultivate a motivated independence in my own learning that has followed me to this day. Had these individuals acted out of a lack of care and attention to protocol, the aggression of the majority of my peers and a few in positions of authority might have overwhelmed me.

Mentorship is not a formula to help those self-identified as leaders succeed, or a platform for others who have succeeded to indoctrinate the next generation. It is a human right in all of the scenarios in which we collide in community—occupational, educational, and informal. I have been mentored by people I accidentally almost injured while learning to surf, by neighbors who noticed that I was installing skylights with a less than effective kind of caulk, by acquaintances in activist communities who saw my hesitation to contribute to dialogue out of fear of saying the wrong thing. I have been mentored in professional settings to recognize gifts I didn't know I possessed, and to correct behaviors that were negatively affecting my colleagues or preventing me from contributing fully to the effort at hand. I have been mentored by coworkers, employees, bosses, students, friends, family members, and strangers: at the core of all of these interactions was a simple willingness of one individual to skillfully extend themselves in order to positively facilitate the process or experience of another. In kind, I consciously try—particularly in the workplace—to identify opportunities to engage in this most necessary and empowering of reciprocal relationships.

Re: Support, ask yourself: Do I mentor and seek mentorship? Have I clearly identified and expressed appreciation for those who have supported me along my trajectory? Do I seek to identify the skills and potential in all of those I work with and for, and devote equivalent energy to helping all of them self-actualize? If I manage others, am I directing their efforts as an extension of my own goals, or am I helping them become more confident/competent/skillful?

Elasticity

In order to lead, you must be able to flex. I can think of countless situations over the positions I've held in which things did not go as planned, failed miserably, and/or proved themselves unsustainable. I can think of as many crucible situations in which I was challenged to try or learn something utterly new, scared out of my mind that I wouldn't be able to pull it off, only to find that even if I didn't, it was an experience that left me more pliable and realistic (and often more confident). Elasticity in the leadership sense is the ability to not be hamstrung by the unexpected, to not freeze or automatically defer/demur when confronted with a task that appears out of your comfort zone. These moments are absolutely inevitable, particularly when work is new or unfamiliar—that is, the reality in which we all operate. These are also the moments that prevent people from applying for new positions, going for grants and awards, presenting in high-stakes situations, or reaching out to someone who might hold the key to an important initiative.

The beginning of anything is stressful, but the knowledge that one is capable of adapting to new situations with grace can be extremely liberating. This is unfortunately not innate in most people—rather, it is *learned*. My most vivid experience of this sort of elasticity was in learning how to teach, a daunting task that I did not realize I was signing up for when I decided to pursue librarianship. Impostor syndrome is an absolute nightmare when facing down a group of unfamiliar students, yet it was this painful process of trial and error that taught me the most about stretching myself in directions I did not know were possible or even advisable. Over years of diligent inquiry into best practices and strategies on the ground, I grew to love the act of teaching and became passionate about encouraging this love in others. Moreover, this process taught me not to cling too tightly to one picture of myself and what I was "supposed to" be doing, that I had a great deal of agency in directing the course of my own career if only I could compel myself to evolve.

Inflexibility often stems from self-doubt, and always poisons personal growth. A hallmark of rigidity in leaders is projecting an aura of abject proficiency, which acts as an armor against vulnerability. The fear of being perceived as less than capable can insulate you from the knowledge and expertise of others, which has a way of inhibiting creativity and collegiality through isolation. Admitting that you have much to learn is as emancipatory as it is disarming, and developing effective strategies for adaptation is essential—these are the hallmarks of professional perseverance.

Re: Elasticity, ask yourself: How do I deal with the unfamiliar? Am I capable of pushing myself toward situations in which I know I will not be able to get by with a pro forma performance? What is my reaction to realizing that I have significant knowledge gaps related to my work, and what have I taken from situations in which I did not succeed in precisely the way I wanted to?

Conclusion

At its simplest and most effective, leadership is to act fearlessly from a motivating purpose that can be articulated with conviction, and to dismantle external and internal barriers to taking effective personal action toward a larger vision. The expression of leadership should affect others positively, inspire and compel others toward action, and result in far more than illumination by cachet. To be a leader you must develop the ability to help others see new tones and shapes in a familiar picture, to think and work with greater conviction, to recognize, confront, and adapt to problems that exist on the ground.

Leadership is not success, power, or bragging rights. It is not ruthlessness, ambition, opportunism, or acquisitiveness. Most of all it is not the opposite of followership. It is empowerment, the identification and principled dismantling of personal and professional barriers in service of a greater good. It is the systematic challenging of self and others to do better, to bring a broader perspective to what can so often feel like the confining context of work. It is identifying a core underlying conviction and allowing it to guide your judgment, decisions, and collaborations. It is challenging the lure of silence and inaction by sharing ideas and opinions that might lead to something more or different. It is creating the conditions for agency and self-realization, not in isolation but in community. It is the activation of *voice*.

////////// **REFLECTIONS: KEY LESSONS FOR LEADERS**

» Consider your relationship to *leadership* as a concept, and alternatively as a basis for action. Do you critically analyze any conflicts or barriers that exist between the two?

» Personal experiences can deeply inform professional convictions, and in so doing create a more powerful basis for advocacy. What aligns the personal and professional in your own experience?

» The qualities of conviction, vision, support, and elasticity can have a powerful impact on the way one works. How do they factor into your professional trajectory?

12

CULTIVATING CONNECTIONS: LEADING THE PURSUIT FOR GREATER LIBRARY ENGAGEMENT

Brian Mathews

////////////// TOP TAKEAWAYS IN THIS CHAPTER

» Focus on advancing the interests and pursuits of the local population rather than being driven to increase library transactions

» Librarianship should be entwined with the usage and comprehension of information, not just discovery

» Strive to work horizontally across your organization, not vertically up-and-down within your department

Building Relationships

"I just helped two people in the hallway; looks like I'm in the lead again!" This playful taunt came from my supervisor as he poked his head into my office. I was a brand-new librarian working at the George Washington (GW) University's satellite campus (focused on graduate research in science and technology) located near Dulles Airport in Virginia. My title was Reference and Instruction Librarian but the job was very unique. We didn't have a reference desk and we did very little formal classroom instruction. There were no dorms and very few faculty were around; it's a commuter campus with no captive audience. In order to have an impact I needed to find creative ways to engage the community. This experience taught me to be resourceful. I had to take the library out to the people. In those early years I operated similarly to a salesman going door-to-door (office-to-office, classroom-to-classroom, lab-to-lab) trying to promote the library wherever I could. I sent countless e-mails, made many cold calls, and designed and distributed handfuls of flyers.

I realized that you could become a great library expert but that it takes more effort to build clientele. To be successful I needed to establish relationships.

I did everything I could imagine to promote the library, but often it was a hard sell. It was difficult pinning people down or explaining the full suite of services we made available. I adapted my methods over time and moved more toward operating like an ambassador. I still represented the library first and foremost, but my energy was increasingly invested in understanding the activities and perspectives of the campus community. I focused on advancing the interests and pursuits of the local population rather than being driven to increase library transactions. For example, instead of handing out flyers or sending e-mails about library services, I started walking around and asking questions. I wondered: how could I help people be more effective and efficient?

This shift of effort ultimately did result in more transactions, just of a different nature. Many times I helped people identify books or locate conference papers, but I also brainstormed methodologies and dissertation topics, judged debates, and tested software prototypes. I also found myself applying emotional intelligence by offering encouragement to students who felt frustrated with assignments or with their programs.

While library school helped me become an information professional, I found that I also needed to develop my interpersonal skills in order to connect with my community. I realized that you could become a great library expert but that it takes more effort to build clientele. To be successful I needed to establish relationships. I had to think beyond answering reference questions, teaching information literacy skills, or managing collections. I had to immerse myself in the daily life of the campus.

The Trusted Advisor is a book that had a profound effect on me. It argues that we should not be satisfied with just providing excellent service, but rather, we should ascend to earn trust and build credibility with the objective of developing relationships. In this sense, we ascend to a higher level of esteem (and utilization) when we transcend beyond technical and subject expertise, and are then viewed in terms of our ability to put issues into context and provide ideas and perspective. I thought that because I was a librarian, people would automatically trust me with their information needs and hold me in high esteem in such matters, but I found that I needed to work hard to explain just how a librarian could fit into their work cycles.

This philosophy expanded my outlook and led to different types of interactions. I sat with physicists editing their papers. I engaged with students and staff in stairwells, the cafeteria, and the campus gym. I discussed teaching and research with faculty in the parking lot as well as at the local golf course. I was in constant pursuit of conversations rather than just reference transactions.

My boss kept track of his encounters as a way to document the boutique services we provided. Keeping pace with him was my motivation. Each day was an experiment pushing my social tact. This position taught me to be agile, open-minded, adventurous, and holistic. These qualities are integral to my career.

Becoming Project Oriented

After a few years at GW, I took a position at Georgia Tech. Reference and instruction duties were once again the cornerstone but I also served as the coordinator for distance learning services. This was my first formal leadership position. I spent a lot time troubleshooting online access problems (firewalls, proxy issues, etc.) as well as promoting library services to students across the globe. (Note: this was in the era before EZproxy when Internet browsers required manual configuration for remote access to library materials.) I advised instructors about online tools and worked closely with librarians to help them in digital environments. In this role I also represented the library in some campus-wide discussions. Our many conversations about the future of online pedagogy and the development of new international locations furthered my thinking on how librarians can help their institutions grow.

Learning the Language. When I arrived at Georgia Tech I quickly identified a big gap in my knowledge: chemistry. This was a critical moment of self-awareness as I perceived a lack in my skill set that was an impediment to my practice. I'd never taken a course in the subject and I struggled with it at the reference desk. Chemistry was connected with many disciplines and if I wanted to establish credibility with scientists and engineers, I needed to learn more. So, during my first year I taught myself the basics. I read, watched videos, attended a few class sessions, and worked on problem sets. I also benefited from great mentoring by my colleagues.

After that year I could perform structure searches in SciFinder and talk with engineers about tribology, fatigue, and IR spectroscopy. My goal was to develop a working knowledge of the discipline. I view this as another form of leadership. I needed to learn their language in order to join their conversations. To be helpful, I needed to understand material properties so that I could offer research suggestions or even understand the questions they were asking. This basic reality taught me that librarianship should be entwined with the usage and comprehension of information, not just storage, licensing, and discovery.

Context. Another valuable lesson I learned was customizing context for the audience. A computer science professor once invited me to his class to talk about Safari Books Online. As I demonstrated the interface and many of the advanced features, I could see the students were bored. It didn't matter how enthusiastic I was or how practical the application—I just wasn't connecting.

This made me rethink my approach to instruction and I decided to try something different: an online community. I chose a weekly theme (security, net neutrality, online ethics, etc.) and recruited a guest (typically a professor or graduate student) to join me for the evening session. We talked about the topic at hand and any related current news. Throughout this optional 90-minute session I would weave in information about relevant library services or resources. Toward the end of these digital meet-ups, students began sharing about their assignments and personal projects. Unexpectedly, I had created a platform that supported mentoring and advising. This taught me about the value of intrinsically motivated learning and the power of a community of practice.

Assessment. Assessment is another area in which librarians can build influence. Understanding users and linking library interactions to strategic outcomes is a powerful capability. For me this started with LibQUAL+ where I was drawn to decoding the data set. What were people trying to tell us about the library? I recall feeling proud at composing a handout for the library's management team. I presented them with examples of gap analysis, standard deviation scores, and lots of other beautifully abstract findings. They looked at me strangely. It dawned on me that this was another instance when context was crucial. They just wanted to know which areas were going well and which ones needed attention.

This LibQUAL+ experience started me on a path of benchmarking my library with its peers. Were others doing things differently, resulting in higher satisfaction ratings? One example I uncovered involved study rooms. Libraries that offered reservable rooms often had more positive scores related to group collaboration. Mining the data in this manner was useful for planning and reviewing our practices. As I focused more on understanding the performance of our organization, I found that I could extend my leadership by talking to the staff about how our policies, practices, and attitudes shaped the way people used (and felt about) the library.

Projects Build Experience. While working at Georgia Tech I had many opportunities to serve on a variety of committees and task forces. I started to pay more attention to the composition of groups. Why did some efforts turn out more smoothly than others? What was my role and what roles did others play? Was the outcome different with a micromanager compared to someone more laissez-faire? How did we handle conflict? Did we celebrate success? These were formative years. I experienced many accomplishments but also several setbacks and miscommunications. I learned that things never go as planned and that it is important to accept that and built it into workflows. Georgia Tech taught me to be agile. You can read a lot about management and leadership but until you encounter different styles and circumstances, certain nuances are impossible to comprehend or appreciate fully.

Probably my most significant takeaway was the necessity of establishing expectations. Projects worked better when everyone involved understood their responsibilities and we collectively formed a clear idea of what we were trying to do. Having a shared outcome made a crucial difference during debates or exploratory discussions; we could always come back to our central purpose to help guide our direction and decision making.

User Experience. My work on various projects in the library and across campus led to a new position at Georgia Tech: user experience librarian. To my knowledge this was the first position of its kind in the United States. I later discovered that another librarian from a Canadian university had the same title a few months before me, but her work focused on Web environments.

My vision for this position blended together marketing, outreach, and assessment with social media, Web design, learning commons development, and public services. It was an evolution of what I had started at George Washington: viewing the library through the eyes (and emotions) of our users and seeking ways to make things better for them.

I turned to user-centered design and ethnography to help structure my work and expand my way of seeing the world. These tools gave me the mindset to consider how everything is connected and interdependent. All of our spaces, services, resources, and policies work together in unison. I viewed my job as *hacking* that system so we could operate more effectively and help the organization have a greater impact. In this leadership role I served as a consultant, studying problems and designing new approaches. I worked hand-in-hand with many different people.

Today I describe this as working horizontally across the entire organization as opposed to vertically, where the focus is on one unit. So instead of working for the reference department, I could move seamlessly between access services, technical services, IT, or special collections. My strategy mimicked the user journey, which typically involves interactions across multiple parts of the library. Cultivating maximum flexibility in this position, I broke through silos and operated beyond traditional boundaries. For example, I was able to bring different units (with different perspectives and priorities) together to work on a new group commons in the library and to figure out shared responsibilities.

During this time a marketer from Georgia Tech's public relations team offered some wisdom. She advised me to look for things that no one else is doing and then to focus on becoming great at doing whatever that was. The entrepreneurial world calls this looking for *white space,* or open areas that are underdeveloped. This philosophy strongly resonated with me, and I saw at once that libraries could be very different things to different people. We limit ourselves if we pigeonhole our role, because our communities need us to evolve and adapt with them. Sometimes they might need a book or article, and other times help using a research tool. But sometimes they need a partner, a confidant, an idea, or just permission to brainstorm. It was at this point that I appreciated that patrons form unique and emotional relationships with their libraries, and that our efforts could propel them to accomplish things they otherwise would be unable to do.

Becoming Program Oriented

My next professional opportunity took me to California. I became an assistant university librarian at the University of California, Santa Barbara (UCSB). This more programmatic role combined outreach initiatives and academic services. Instead of launching projects or examining internal processes, I was responsible for operations across a larger scope. For example, instead of just thinking about enhancing student orientation, I considered the entire first-year experience: helping students transition from high school and supporting their emotional and intellectual growth during that formative period.

As a user experience librarian at Georgia Tech, I operated as a free agent: working with anyone on anything. This position at UCSB placed me into my first administrative role. I now served on an executive team making strategic decisions about the organization.

Crucible Moment #1: Budget Crisis. Within weeks of moving out west in 2008 I faced my first major crucible moment. The economy tanked and UC suffered a massive budget cut. Tuition was raised 33 percent. Employees were furloughed. Regular protests and sit-ins occurred across the entire UC system. Some of these resulted in violence. It was an extremely stressful time for everyone and an especially challenging environment in which to start as an administrator. I doubted my decision to leave Georgia Tech, where things were stable and we had recently earned the ACRL Excellence Award. All across UC, I encountered stories of anger, sadness, confusion, and suspicion. We were operating in survival mode. Academic units were downsizing and looking for ways to make cuts. It was within this emotionally charged climate that I had to lead change and help move the library forward.

All across the campus people were feeling down and I wanted to position the library as a positive force at UCSB. One of the first things I did was work closely with Student Affairs and many student organizations. We shaped the library as a gathering space for events, exhibits, and other activities. I wanted us to become a place where students and faculty could bond. I wanted the library to be an intellectual and unifying spark on our campus.

One asset that we had was a common book program managed by the library. Each year we gave away thousands of books so that students and faculty across the curriculum could have a shared experience. While many colleges incorporate similar initiatives into the first-year programs, ours was a much wider effort that included upper-level courses and partnerships with the local public library and a neighboring community college.

I made the decision to form a campus-wide library board to garner greater buy-in. We needed students, staff, and faculty to feel ownership of the program, rather than it remaining library-driven. I wanted others to be responsible for its success and guide us in new directions. I feel that the common book program was therapeutic for many people. It brought together different courses and different disciplines to examine broad themes such as sustainability, immigration, and ethics. We used reading, discussions, lectures, and interactive activities as a platform for exploring ideas, emotions, and opportunities to change the world.

Bringing the Library Together. While I worked to create bonding moments for the campus, I needed to foster a positive experience for our employees as well. One of the more challenging tasks I had was overseeing the migration of the library's Web site from a loose assortment of HTML pages into a shared content management system.

Our approach to Web content had been decentralized, and it showed with a very inconsistent Web presence. It would take both technical and social proficiency to bring everyone together.

While we wanted the site to have a cohesive look and feel, we actually started with its words. We needed to get on the same page (so to speak) in terms of our vocabulary and resolve differences such as standardizing our usage of "ebook," "eBook," "e-book," and "electronic book." After establishing a common language we proofread every sentence on every page. Like many libraries, we developed wireframes and mock-ups. We shared these with library personnel and took them on usability tests all across campus. We spent months gathering feedback that helped shape our progress. In a small way, I like to think that we brought a positive experience to a campus enduring troubling times: a chance to reflect and foster some constructive engagement.

Our cross-departmental Web team had a little over a year to complete the migration. I had recently read *Sacred Hoops: Spiritual Lessons of a Hardwood Warrior* by legendary basketball coach Phil Jackson. He describes his leadership through the act of assembling teams and managing their personalities. I was inspired by his story and wanted to use his approach for our Web team journey. Maybe because I was a new administrator, I felt the need to push out a lofty vision or to make things more complicated than they needed to be. I eventually saw in myself, and I've witnessed in others, the need to prove something and assert control rather than just focusing on what the group needs in order to thrive. During our kickoff meeting I mentioned Phil Jackson and compared our work to that of a basketball team at the start of a season. Each person possessed different abilities and perspectives and we needed to work together to have success. *Silence.*

Was the sports analogy a problem? Was I unclear? Did I rush it? What I was trying to get across was that some of them were coders, while others had strong writing abilities or design skills. A few were new to the profession, while some had decades of institutional knowledge. We also had many library departments represented, as well as a student on the team. I probably should have just said that, but I felt the need to wrap it around a metaphor. Next I suggested that we were like an orchestra, with each person playing a different instrument and coming together in harmony. *More silence.*

How could I connect with them? I think this is a challenge that many new leaders face. Arriving at a place as an outsider and having to navigate your way through existing, often long-standing, relationships. I felt I needed to prove myself and earn their trust, so I made one more attempt and suggested that we could be like the Beatles. The Web site was our album—our canvas— and it would take all of us working together to make it great. They were quiet but then someone responded: "That could work, as long as it's not the *White Album.*" *Laughter.* She was referencing the record where the band fell apart with conflict and creative differences. The team went on to meet its deadline and we all felt proud of our effort. It was a good lesson for me, not only in thinking on my feet, but also in terms of overthinking my role. Perhaps I should have led an exercise where I let them form an identity together rather than trying to force one upon them?

Inclusion. At UCSB I had another mishap that led to an important leadership lesson. I established a partnership with the Graduate Division to hire a Ph.D. candidate to conduct some ethnographic work. We designed a project that included interviews and field studies aimed at better understanding the graduate student population at the university. At the time, UCSB had about 900 graduate students compared to 18,000 undergraduates.

This effort launched with all the best intentions. It took us all across campus, from music halls and painting studios to nano labs and materials testing facilities. We even Web-conferenced with one student conducting marine research on a remote Pacific island. The students appreciated that we were taking the time to ask them questions about their work and lives. Many of them thanked us for showing interest and collecting their stories. We were able to get a better sense of the graduate landscape and to observe how different academic departments functioned. We also identified opportunities for both the library and the campus to better assist this population. The problem was that I didn't involve enough people. I was trying to get our assessment program off the ground and took on a lot of the responsibility myself. I used the ethnography project as a chance for me to learn more about the campus but I should have involved the liaisons more closely. Maybe forming a steering committee or even a regular informal group to review the incoming data would have been sufficient. Librarians and others were interested in our results but I didn't give them enough opportunities to engage during the gathering process.

My underuse of greater internal collaboration is something I would learn from going forward. While I had made strides to better understand the campus community, I had missed out on strengthening the community within the library. While we identified some potential new initiatives, I feel the librarians and staff might have connected more with the findings (and felt greater encouragement to implement new efforts) if they had been more involved throughout the project.

Becoming Culture Oriented

My next, and current, leadership position promoted me to an associate dean at Virginia Tech. The first challenge I faced was developing a plan to renovate the library. The space was outdated and had a bland institutional feel. I spent the first year just talking with people about what we needed to do.

I reached back into the user experience tool kit and assembled something I called "discovery teams." These were small groups that explored broad themes, such as collaboration, technology, media production, and individual work. Each team conducted a handful of interviews, took photos, and recorded other observations related to their topic. My objective was twofold. I wanted to get a sense of the campus and the work that students were doing. And second, I wanted to create an opportunity for library employees and others across campus to feel included in the process.

We had nearly 50 volunteers sign up. People who typically didn't work together were encouraged to have a shared experience and to see the campus through our students' eyes. They spent time in different parts of the library, as well as in classrooms, student centers, media labs, residential areas, and outdoors. One team even visited a local bar to observe "group dynamics" in action. Most people had fun with the exercise and their reports and insights informed our thinking going forward. Along with the discovery teams, we worked with architects and interior designers on developing some concepts. We hosted many interviews, focus groups, and design charrettes, as well as reviewed LibQUAL+ and other data streams. I met with many campus groups and committees to gather feedback and validate our findings. We generated a lot of interest and developed a clear sense of the direction in which the library needed grow. In the end we hired a firm to produce schematic drawings based on this effort and slowly initiated some renovations.

Crucible Moment #2: Faculty Resistance. It was after all this work when another crucible moment emerged. I took our insights and prototypes to various Faculty Senate meetings. By this time the brainstorming and analysis phase was complete and we were presenting our path forward.

At one meeting a senior faculty member interjected and said he wished to play devil's advocate. He proceeded to berate the library collection and argued that what we really needed were more microfilm holdings and not a learning commons. His hostility caught me off guard. I wasn't sure how to respond. His tone was so negative that it silenced the room. No one else said anything. When he finished I thanked him for his feedback and that was the end of it.

I took this exchange very personally. I was disappointed with myself that I didn't have a better response. I felt discouraged that we had invested so much time engaging the campus, and here our effort was being dismissed. Could I have done more as a leader? This helped me realize that, as an administrator, I also needed to be a politician and learn to stay on message.

As this meeting lingered with me I started noticing the same theme elsewhere. There are many stories of libraries undergoing substantial changes and encountering resistance from faculty. Some disciplines are not funded as well as others, and I think this can result in bitterness. Librarians sometimes take the brunt of this dissatisfaction.

I've since realized that the professor was not attacking me but expressing his frustration with historical problems and other changes happening around him. He used the opportunity to make a symbolic gesture on the seeming priority of undergraduate needs at the expense of faculty. This was an opportunity for me to practice empathic thinking, seeing the situation from another person's perspective. This helped moving forward as I started including messages about new services and spaces created to help faculty with their teaching and research endeavors.

The way that I have processed this and similar conversations is that when people are upset with the library, it is usually because they want to see it improve. This encouraged me to return my focus back to relationship building: trying to turn dissidence into advocacy. We need passionate faculty on our side, pushing for specialized collections, spaces, and research services. We need them to understand our difficulties, and likewise, we need to appreciate their problems and expectations as well. This shift from defending the library to building alliances has resulted in broader support and deeper interest in our work. This faculty encounter, although awkward at the time, helped me realize that I needed to have responses ready for challenging questions or provocative statements. I needed to be able to articulate our intentions and benefits using non-librarian language. I had to link what we are doing to the larger changes across campus related to pedagogy and research. Ultimately, you can be as prepared as possible, but until you get battle tested in the field, your ability to anticipate and respond to such a confrontation is uncertain.

Progress. We've made steady progress across the Virginia Tech Libraries in upgrading our commons areas and classrooms and hiring for positions that add new expertise. Our gate count numbers rose from less than 500,000 annual visitors to 1.3 million in a matter of years. People are excited about the library and we are gaining respect. Our growing reputation is evident in the Provost's Office inviting us to co-chair a campus-wide effort to develop commons areas all across the university, which affords us an opportunity to export our knowledge of learning environments to a broader audience. This is another form of leadership: shaping experiences that will impact thousands of students each semester. While we obviously want to enhance the condition of the library, our mission, ultimately, is to improve the university as a whole.

Restructuring. I have one final leadership story to share. This one is about organizational change. We had a number of simultaneous retirements and staff resignations. As we considered these vacancies, we saw the potential for realigning our organization to better match our strategic vision. I took on the task of bringing four units together into a new and more cohesive division.

I was excited about this chance to start from scratch. Similar to migrating the Web site at UCSB, this was an opportunity to bring people together on a path leading in a new direction. I appointed a management team and we worked for two months on changes. After interviewing everyone who would be impacted, we prepared for the transition. We invested a lot of effort and empathy into anticipating how people would feel and understood that this was more than just a functional change. For many people, their job is linked to their identity. Even though we knew this was about positive change, it was disruptive nonetheless. My managers spent an enormous amount of time connecting with people one-on-one and working hard to build a sense of team unity.

My leadership lesson from this change-making experience was that I needed to rely on good advice and insight from my department heads. We all need people with different perspectives and management styles to ensure we are being fully considerate during times of change. It is easy to develop tunnel vision, focusing solely on what you want to achieve. But the danger is that you could miss critical elements, detrimental to success, if you are leading blindly. I found that I needed to place full trust in my leadership team who understood how each of their staff would react and who could help me see potential pitfalls in my thinking.

Continuous Improvement. I've started to move more toward lean management philosophies. One of the general concepts is that people impacted by a change should be involved with shaping it. I wanted to encourage a sense of empowerment by including employees in the process so that they are the ones advocating for change, which in turn leads them to be more supportive of its success. Each semester we make small tweaks to positions, policies, reporting lines, and so forth based on what we learned the previous term. We are vigilant about missed opportunities so we can make improvements in the future.

Lean strategies give us tools to help the people who are the closest to the action. We aspire to give them the freedom to improvise, notice problems, and address changes that could help us become more effective. As leaders, we give them support, encouragement, and a sense of responsibility. We view it as everyone's job to fix what's broken and take ownership of problems rather than expect that someone else will deal with it. In fact, we put this notion in their position descriptions. Everyone is empowered to help create the conditions that can nurture excellent experiences for our students, faculty, and other library members.

Agility. A few years ago I wrote a paper titled "Think Like A Startup." The main point I tried to make was that libraries could learn a lot from these fledgling companies. I wasn't implying that we needed to adapt their business models or that we should toss aside our legacy, but rather, like them, we are organizations undergoing constant change and facing a degree of uncertainty about our future. Libraries, like their parent institutions, are increasingly more accountable for their spending, staff, and outcomes. We have to articulate a better sense of value and demonstrate not only good stewardship but also innovative thinking that can help our institutions move forward. We can learn a lot from others engaged in similar efforts.

The start-up metaphor worked for me. I view it as a call to be proactive and optimistic. Our effort is strengthened when we realize that the work we're doing and the work ahead is centered on constant change, not on old benchmarks of excellence. All leaders in higher education would benefit from learning how to shift priorities, pivot programs, and adjust on the fly as new circumstances emerge.

We will be redefining libraries in the decades to come. What are they? What are they becoming? What will they enable people to do? Agility is a critical attribute for leaders. By staying grounded in a desire to connect with our communities and help them become more successful, librarianship remains on a positive path that will take us in many new and different directions. To get us on that path and keep us there, we need librarians and staff to accept leadership responsibility at every level of our organizations and to work at constantly improving the experience for users and our fellow colleagues alike.

REFLECTIONS: KEY LESSONS FOR LEADERS

» We must push ourselves beyond excellent service, aspiring and ascending to earn trust and build credibility with the objective of developing relationships

» Extend leadership by framing conversations that help shape the strategy of the organization

» Projects work better when everyone understands their responsibilities

» We need librarians and staff to accept leadership responsibility at every level of our organizations and constantly to work at improving the experience

References

Bell, Steven, and John Shank. *Academic Librarianship by Design: A Blended Librarian's Guide to the Tools and Techniques.* Chicago: American Library Association, 2007.

Dennis, Pascal, and Jim Womack. *Getting the Right Things Done: A Leader's Guide to Planning and Execution.* Cambridge, MA: Lean Enterprise Institute, 2006.

"Designing Thinking for Libraries." http://designthinkingforlibraries.com (Accessed June 2015).

Dorney, Erin. "The User Experience Librarian." *College and Research Library News* (June 2009). http://crln.acrl.org/content/70/6/346.full.pdf (Accessed June 2015).

Foster, Nancy Fried, and Susan Gibbons. *Studying Students: The Undergraduate Research Project at the University of Rochester.* Chicago: ACRL Publications, 2007.

Jackson, Phil. *Sacred Hoops: Spiritual Lessons of a Hardwood Warrior.* New York: Hyperion, 1995.

Maister, David, Charles Green, and Robert Galford. *The Trusted Advisor.* New York: Free Press, 2000.

Mathews, Brian. "Think Like a Start-Up: a White Paper." The Ubiquitous Librarian Blog. *Chronicle of Higher Education* (April 4, 2012). http://chronicle.com/blognetwork/theubiquitouslibrarian/2012/04/04/think-like-a-startup-a-white-paper (Accessed June 2015).

Mathews, Brian. "The Virtual Reality: Exploring Graduate Student Use Patterns of the UCSB Library." The Ubiquitous Librarian Blog. *Chronicle of Higher Education* (May 2, 2011). http://chronicle.com/blognetwork/theubiquitouslibrarian/2011/05/02/the-virtual-reality-exploring-graduate-student-use-patterns-of-the-ucsb-library (Accessed June 2015).

Miller, Rebecca. "Individual Adaptation: Interdisciplinary Perspectives on Personal Identity and Learning During Organizational Change." Association of College and Research Libraries (ACRL) Conference Paper, March 2015. http://www.ala.org/acrl/sites/ala.org.acrl/files/content/conferences/confsandpreconfs/2015/Miller.pdf (Accessed June 2015).

Rother, Mike. *Toyota Kata: Managing People for Improvement, Adaptiveness and Superior Results.* New York: McGraw-Hill, 2010.

Unger, Russ, and Carolyn Chandler. *A Project Guide to UX Design: For User Experience Designers in the Field or in the Making.* Berkeley, CA: New Riders/ Pearson Education, 2009.

—— 13 ——

NO FIRE. NO NUDITY. GOOD GRAMMAR.

Erin T. Smith

/////////////// TOP TAKEAWAYS IN THIS CHAPTER

» Learn the power of saying "Yes"
» Don't dismiss internal promotion as a path to leadership opportunities
» When your vision requires external support, ask before you leap
» Forget tradition and follow the need
» Strategic planning can be a group process
» Give difficult employees your respect and empathy, but not control
» Keep moving forward

Three Simple Rules for Leading a Library

At the end of my first year as library director of a small liberal arts college, one of my librarians was thinking about ways to ramp up our use of social media in order to increase student engagement during the following year. She recruited a small group of student workers to generate some YouTube content during the summer. The first idea the students came up with was a Harry Potter floo powder spoof. "Great!" my colleague said, "Just no actual fire in the library." The second idea was to shoot a Harlem Shake video in the library computer lab. "Love it!" I said, "Just make sure everyone is fully clothed." The third idea . . . well, to be honest, I can't remember the actual content of the third idea, but it involved a student-produced meme that required some serious editing to make sure that nouns and verbs were in agreement.

Since that summer those three things—no fire, no nudity, good grammar—have stood as a mantra for my library staff. It's shorthand for describing our willingness to try almost anything with library spaces, services, and resources that might engage our campus. It's also indicative of my leadership philosophy: start with a "yes." I never intended to be a library director, much less to serve in my current capacity as an Associate Dean overseeing both library and information technology (IT) functionality. In fact, I didn't even set out to be a librarian. However, when interesting opportunities are presented to me, my first instinct is to pursue them to see what might happen.

A Reluctant Librarian

As a graduate student in a Masters of Information Science (MIS) program, I planned to go into academic publishing, not academic librarianship. During my senior year of college, the director of the university press urged me to consider a program in digital publishing offered through the School of Information Science at the University of Tennessee (UT), saying the experience would make me stand head and shoulders above all the English majors I would be competing against for entry-level positions in the publishing field. I applied and was accepted to the program; however, with weeks before classes were to begin I learned that the digital publishing track had been discontinued. I decided to go anyway, confident that any master's was better than no master's in the battle for supremacy for the position of mail clerk. The MIS program at UT offered a forward-thinking curriculum that was built on a solid Library Science foundation. The information theory course blew my mind, and my favorite courses focused on information access and retrieval (Thank you, Dialog Classic). I took courses in information representation and collection development. I even did a practicum at a local liberal arts college. But, when asked, I was adamant about going into publishing. I mean, really, I was way too loud to be a librarian. Plus, I didn't own a cat.

It wasn't until I was six months out of graduate school when my best shot at a job at an academic press was dashed by a hiring freeze. That's how I said yes to a position as an academic librarian. As a science reference librarian at the University of Georgia (UGA), I realized that despite the lack of some stereotypical traits, I was actually a pretty good librarian. My favorite patrons were the life science graduate students. They got so excited about finding information and I had a knack for tracking down incomplete or incorrect citations that their dissertation advisers had given them. I loved the relationships I was developing with these repeat patrons and the way they would make a point to come to the library during my shifts on the reference desk.

At UGA, I also said yes to working with the recently hired electronic resources librarian who was charged with getting a handle on licensing models and usage statistics. This e-resource experience helped me land my first permanent position at Westminster College in Pennsylvania, where I said yes to serving as the Cataloging and System Librarian. Or, at least I think that experience is the reason they offered me the job when I had exactly zero experience in either cataloging or library systems.

I spent the next decade at Westminster saying "yes" to lots of things. Yes, I can learn to maintain a server. Yes, I can figure out how to manage our serials. Yes, I'll redesign the library's Web pages. Yes, I'll teach the first-year experience course. Yes, I'll chair that standing faculty committee. And eventually, yes, I'll serve as Director of Library Services.

Duck . . . duck . . . duck . . . duck . . . GOOSE!

In my 10th year at Westminster, the director of the library announced she was going to retire at the end of the year. She made the announcement far in advance in order to provide plenty of time for succession planning. However, the vice president (VP) of Academic Affairs decided not to do a search for a library director, opting instead for appointing me as the new director and authorizing a search for an entry-level librarian. I initially objected to this strategy because I think a lot of my institution and I thought that we deserved the best person on the market. My VP, however, likened it to our long-standing tradition of appointing departmental chairs from the ranks of the faculty. Plus, he said he would always rather work with "the devil he knew."

When you rise to a position of leadership in a place you have worked for a while, there is no honeymoon period. You know there are things that really need to be done that aren't going to be embraced by the library staff. You know the faculty members who are not interested in partnering with the library. You may even have burned some bridges that (it turns out) you really need to move the library forward. Worst of all, there is the danger that you are blind to existing problems because you have become accustomed to current practice.

But there are good things as well. You know the campus culture and have already built a lot of bridges. You know which faculty members are pro-library and the ones who support you personally. You have a list of initiatives to implement and a list of things to phase out. If fact, you may have been secretly dreaming of the day when you would get to chart a new course based on your vision of the library with no expectation that you would actually get to do it. But the biggest benefit I enjoyed with this internal pathway to leadership was an entire year to prepare for my new role. I used that time to tackle the two most important (and interconnected) elements of library administration: the budget and the strategic plan.

The Power of Positive Thinking

Anyone who has ever worked at a small academic library knows the problems that limited resources cause. Despite the addition of new programs and faculty members, the library had only received "cost of living" increases to our budgets during the 10 years I had been there. Worse than that, if we had a year with lower-than-anticipated enrollment, the budget would stay flat or be cut. Due to these limited resources, the previous director was often saying "no." No, I'm sorry but we don't have the budget to add that online resource. No, we cannot extend our hours, we don't have the money to hire additional people. It would be lovely to digitize that collection, but where would we get the money? And it's not because she didn't try to get more money. She faithfully submitted requests for budget increases to fund the acquisition of new resources; however, those requests were just as faithfully denied by the college's administration. She would often wonder why the faculty didn't complain to the administration more viscerally—and why they didn't argue on our behalf because with no additional money in the library budget, there was no way for us to buy the new resources for which they were asking.

> When you rise to a position of leadership in a place you have worked for a while, there is no honeymoon period. You know there are things that really need to be done that aren't going to be embraced by the library staff.

I was not going to continue down this path. In order to start saying yes, I made my last project as online resources and serials librarian an examination of our journal and online resource holdings. For eons, the only way we had been able to add new subscription-based resources was by canceling an existing subscription. This generally happened in the context of a newly hired faculty member who needed a new resource to teach or do research. After receiving a request, I would work with the department with the recent hire to first identify underutilized resources that could be canceled and then to use those savings to invest in the new resource.

I decided to try this approach, which had worked well in a departmental context, with all of our subscription-based resources. I did a massive cost-per-use study and shared it not just with my librarian colleagues but also with departmental faculty. For the faculty, I highlighted underutilized (and therefore unjustifiably expensive) resources and I gave them three options: keep and promote more strongly, cancel and replace with a different disciplinary resource, or cancel and trust the librarians with the savings. To my surprise and delight, many departments chose the third option. We were able to reinvest about 12 percent of our total resource budget just by asking if we could!

Not only were we able to add the resources faculty had been clamoring for, we were also able to invest in resources that our faculty didn't know existed. For example, we implemented a discovery platform that made all of our online resources available from a single search and completely changed the way we taught our beginner information literacy sessions. But, when I look back on that project, the part that was most important to the formation of my leader style was not when I rolled out the new resources; it was when I hit "send" on the e-mail to the departmental faculty sharing less-than-flattering usage statistics and asking that they trust us to do something differently. For it was in that moment that I decided to step out of the library into the crucible, as it were, and to say that I was not going to do things the way they had always been done: I was going to find ways to say yes.

If I Built It, Would They Come?

Another major responsibility new library leaders face is developing and getting support for their vision for the future of the library. For me, the direction was clear: we had to make information literacy (IL) instruction our top priority. I was convinced that IL is essential to student success not only in the academic environment but in life after graduation. I was also acutely aware from our dwindling reference statistics that most undergraduate students do not make the connection between using information well and academic success nor do they understand the value of this skill set beyond writing a research paper. For that reason, when I became director, I wanted us to embrace an active, student-centered approach to IL skill development. I wanted to permanently banish our library tours and orientations in favor of subject-specific, course-integrated IL instruction that is fully integrated with disciplinary student learning outcomes. I wanted a scaffolded approach that introduced increasingly complex IL concepts alongside increasingly complex disciplinary concepts. But to make this happen, it would require a drastic reorganization of the library. We only had four librarians and five paraprofessionals and this kind of change would require a completely new division of labor.

I knew the librarians I worked with were in support of my vision for the future of our library. In fact, even before I officially became the director of McGill Library, we began referring to this change in paradigm as "McGill Library 2.0." But before we tore it all up and started from scratch, I needed to make sure the faculty were also onboard. What if I built programming and services around course-integrated IL instruction, but my colleagues in the classroom didn't see the same need? What if they thought their students used information well and that they didn't need more help? Or what if a majority of the faculty agreed that our students needed something else: a Geographic Information Systems (GIS) lab or archival materials to support a particular element of the curriculum?

To answer these questions, I developed a semi-structured questionnaire and I asked every full-time member of the faculty to meet with me face-to-face to talk about how they ask their students to "find, evaluate, and use information." The interview protocol was designed to solicit the full range of their engagement with information literacy (the concept, not the term). Was it something they thought was important for students? Did they feel their students were lacking competency in this area? If so, would they be interested in working with librarians to help students develop IL competencies? I also asked really broad questions like "What can the library do to best serve the needs of our students?" I dreamed that the vast majority of them would answer that they library would find ways to help our students find better resources. I predicted they would want ridiculously expensive new journal subscriptions in their research fields. I feared they wouldn't be able to conceive of the library doing anything other than collecting resources.

It was in that moment that I decided to step out of the library into the crucible, as it were, and to say that I was not going to do things the way they had always been done: I was going to find ways to say yes.

As a new leader, this was a scary time, a real crucible moment. As a librarian, I had been advocating making IL the center of our mission for years. And now, as the director, I finally had the chance. But what if the faculty saw the library helping in a different way? I wanted to be a bold leader who said yes, but I also wanted to be a wise leader who let our students' actual needs (and not my assumptions about those needs) drive our mission. I decided that whatever I learned from my classroom colleagues, I would design a plan of action to meet the need they described.

Through conversations with almost three-fourths of our faculty, I learned that nearly everyone valued the concepts embodied by the term *information literacy* (even if they didn't know or understand the term itself). I learned that the vast majority of our faculty give assignments that require IL skills in one or more of the courses they teach. I learned that faculty would like to see their students' IL skills improve, particularly as related to the quality of resources students cite in their work. I learned that most faculty had very specific ideas about what they want their students to cite, but that they vary greatly in the lengths they take to communicate those expectations. I learned that many faculty members didn't know we would design IL instruction sessions specifically for their courses and (even better!) for their individual assignments and student learning objectives. I learned that of a significant number of the faculty, the colleagues I worked with on a regular basis didn't know that librarians wanted to work with them in developing the information literacy skills of our students, but said that they were open to the idea. Most importantly, I learned that I had their support for my library vision.

Armed with this knowledge, my colleagues and I got to work on planning the future.

One Vision, Many Voices

Our vision was to create a library in which the development of student IL skills was the top priority. This meant we had to devote less time and resources to acquiring "things" and more time and resources to helping people with their research and information needs. This was, perhaps, not as scary for us as it would be for some. Because of our limited resources, we have always had to contend with the fact that we could not purchase every book or journal "just in case" it might be useful to our users. We have always relied heavily on interlibrary loan and local consortia borrowing agreements. Further, we have always worked closely with our faculty. With only four librarians, we don't have subject specialists in every area so we have a tradition of working closely with faculty in both our collection development and deselection processes. In many regards, this change was just the next logical step.

But that next step was a doozy. We only had four librarians. We knew we were not going to receive an additional position because our request for a new Instructional Librarian had been denied the year before. So, for us, teaching more IL meant figuring out which things we were going to stop doing as a library. Our Research and Instruction Librarian was already teaching a full load. Each of the other three librarians was already working at capacity as well, with two or three areas of responsibility to handle. None of us had the option of just adding more instructional duties to the list of things we were already doing. That next step was a year-long strategic planning process that resulted in a drastic reorganization of library personnel.

In that year, I learned an important lesson in leadership: it is one thing to get support for a vision but quite another to develop and operationalize a strategic plan to make that vision a reality. It was fairly easy for the librarians to reach agreement on the things we wanted to do. In addition to an increased emphasis on information literacy, we also agreed that we needed to provide better online access to library resources and to partner with campus IT to provide instructional support for emerging technologies. But it was downright painful to figure out how to set aside decades of traditions to make it actually happen. This was also the point at which I invited our paraprofessionals to join the discussion.

The involvement of our paraprofessional staff marked a paradigm shift in our library. Previously, only the librarians were involved in decision-making processes. Staff members were often informed of any changes at the point of implementation. However, it was very important to me that everyone who worked in the library have input into the process. The benefit of a small staff is that everyone can participate in a meeting without it being onerous. Every person had a unique piece of the puzzle and we could only see the full picture if everyone shared. I hoped that they would see the new direction for the library as something they were shaping, as opposed to something that was being done to them. Involving them early in the process also made it clear that while I was interested in exploring ways we could change job descriptions, the college's administration wasn't leading this charge. No one was in danger of losing his/her job in the library, so there was no danger in being honest about how busy they were (or were not) or about how worthwhile they thought individual tasks were to the mission of the library. Empowering the entire library staff to influence the strategic planning process of the library not only mitigated some of the pain points other libraries experience during a restructuring process, it also created an inclusive, affirmative environment that has well served every initiative we have tackled since then.

Know When to Hold Them . . . Know When to Walk Away

But to say that this approach made the process full of rainbows and sunshine would be a lie. I was able to negotiate raises for everyone as part of the process, which helped the overall goal. However, I still made some people pretty very unhappy. I made one of the librarians unhappy when I proposed that the only way to make time for more librarians to teach was to reassign some of their responsibilities to our paraprofessionals. The idea of this shift also made a few of our paraprofessionals unhappy. Interestingly, they were okay with the idea of taking on new responsibilities; what they didn't want to do was give up old duties that were suggested for elimination because they ranked lower on the priority list.

For each unhappy person, I tried to offer a spoonful of sugar to help the medicine go down, so to speak. For the unhappy librarian, I tried to keep the focus on the vision, which she passionately supported. I reminded her that, given our situation, using our paraprofessionals differently was the only way we could ramp up our information literacy outreach. For the apprehensive paraprofessional in print periodicals whose entire workload was changing, I tried to sweeten the deal by giving him new responsibilities in an area he was passionate about. The downright disgruntled paraprofessional, who had been unhappy since we changed the circulation desk into a full-service public services desk, was given the opportunity to move into a different position altogether.

Initially, I took these measures to help make the people who weren't fully onboard feel better about the changes. But the real leadership lesson I learned through this process was the importance of working closely with the dissenters to keep them engaged in the planning process while staying true to the vision. This approach was vital to keeping the process going and to the smooth(ish) implementation of the new structure. It also demonstrated to the people who were onboard with changing our priorities that I was not going to sacrifice the good of the library, of the campus, to keep a few people happy.

The Only Constant Is Change

One of the elements of our new vision was to partner with campus IT to provide instructional support for emerging technologies. We were interested in becoming librarians to whom campus community members would turn when they needed help with anything related to information, whether it was searching a database or using an app to organize notes. This idea, which was the furthest stretch of our vision, went from a three-year goal to a one-year goal when my new VP of Academic Affairs (VPAA) blindsided me with a request to design a new organizational structure that would merge the library with campus IT, to serve as Interim Associate Dean of the new unit, and to apply for the permanent position when a national search was conducted later that year. Unlike my appointment as library director a few years earlier, this opportunity wasn't something I had ever even considered. However, as I thought about our vision and of the possibility to merge librarianship with instructional support at the organization level, I decided I had to say yes.

The merger and my appointment as interim of the new unit sent shockwaves through the campus community. Many people sent me messages of congratulations. However, many others sent the VPAA messages that doubted my qualifications to lead IT. Others wondered how I would manage the workload. Some faculty were so upset by the merger itself that they still won't speak to me socially. The fallout from my decision to lead this organizational change was, without a doubt, the most challenging experience of my career. I wasn't accustomed to people questioning my abilities. This was the crucible moment that forced me to look inward. Since other people did not believe in me, I had to believe in myself. And not just in that old *Saturday Night Live* skit when Stuart Smalley would say "I'm good enough, I'm smart enough, and gosh darn it, people like me." I had to believe that I could do more than negotiate licenses for e-resources and develop circulation policies. I had to believe that I was capable of leading not just our information resources forward but also our information technology forward.

But after a year in the role, which included my acceptance of the permanent position after a national search, I have proven that librarians can do more than organize books and that library leadership can prepare a person for success in bigger arenas. In the library, we have long worked closely with our colleagues in IT because we needed their support as we transitioned to online collections and information sources. But libraries also have something of value to offer IT. We understand that students benefit more from learning how to find and evaluate information than they do from our just handing them an article on their topic. Our students would benefit just as much from learning how to do malware scans on their own laptops, instead of us just doing it all for them. Just as the changing technological landscape opened up new possibilities for access to information that could not be imagined in a print-based scholarly communication system,

I learned an important lesson in leadership: it is one thing to get support for a vision but quite another to develop and operationalize a strategic plan to make that vision a reality.

new opportunities now exist in instructional and workplace/productivity technologies as free and low-cost applications are introduced as viable alternatives to traditional (and expensive) enterprise-wide solutions.

Serving as Associate Dean of Library and Information Services means I have the opportunity to think about the interconnectedness of information resources and information technology. I also have the opportunity to develop new models of service in which both the library and our IT services are directly connected, in philosophy and services, to what is happening in the curriculum. On our campus, with our new merged department, the library is not only the place where people come when they need to find some information, it's the place they come when they need help with information technology. With this merger, and with my colleagues' decision to put a librarian at the helm of Library & Information Services, I really feel like we are well on our way to the next iteration of reimagining the academic library.

And with no fire, no nudity, and good grammar as our criteria, there's no telling how far we'll go.

///////////// REFLECTIONS: KEY LESSONS FOR LEADERS

» Be open and flexible: it will lead to opportunities you could never imagine

» From beginning to end, be as inclusive as possible when leading change

» Despite your best efforts, some people won't buy into your vision; don't let them win

» If you aren't taking risks, then you aren't really leading

14

NAVIGATING CHOPPY WATERS: CATALYSTS FOR SMOOTH LEADERSHIP SAILING

Eboni A. Johnson

TOP TAKEAWAYS IN THIS CHAPTER

» Use failure or near-failure as a catalyst for positive growth

» Face your fears—amazing things rarely happen inside your comfort zone

» Use your work philosophy as a guiding light to building your professional legacy

> I am not afraid of storms, for I am learning how to sail my ship.
>
> —LOUISA MAY ALCOTT

It is difficult for me to think myself a leader in the library profession. I feel that I'm just doing my job. I've been a professional for well over a decade and have worked in libraries in various capacities since high school. Unlike several other librarians I've talked to over the years, I deliberately chose librarianship as my career. But when I've thought about library leaders in the past, I always pictured them serving as deans, directors, department heads, or officers of professional associations—high-profile positions to which I had never aspired. When I was a librarian-in-training and I daydreamed about the course my career might take, I pictured myself as a no-frills reference librarian from the day I earned my MLIS until the day I retired. What I didn't know until quite recently is that I could be that kind of librarian and still be a leader in the profession. I also didn't know that it would take what I consider a near-failure in my career to bring this change about.

Adrift

While library leaders often recognize the occurrences that represent their own crucible moments, they may not realize how their interactions with staff, both positive and negative, may also evolve into crucible moments for staff members. When leaders fail to live up to their responsibility to provide adequate and constructive feedback, opportunities for professional development and career advancement, and so on, these actions may serve as a catalyst for that staff member to change—to change positions, to change employers, or even to change careers. I have experienced negativity at various times in my career, as I'm sure many of us have—unsupportive supervisors, mean-spirited coworkers, toxic work environments. What do you do in situations where a negative interaction, or a series of them, shakes you off balance and causes you to question your skills and abilities? Great leaders have the capacity to separate themselves from negative acts; to look at the situation(s) critically, yet objectively; and to decide to move forward from them in a positive way. All of this may be easier said than done, particularly when vulnerability and pride can play such large roles in our ability to face adverse situations and overcome them.

I have been incredibly fortunate to have had mentors help me navigate some choppy waters along my career path. As a new tenure-track librarian at a large research institution, I was being groomed to take over as head of one of the campus libraries upon the incumbent librarian's retirement; this succession planning was built into my position. While my annual performance reviews noted that I was "exceeding expectations" in my day-to-day work as interim head of a department library—specifically faculty engagement, instruction, collection development and management, outreach and publicity, and staff supervision, the research and publication part of my portfolio was progressing far more slowly. I had a hard time vigorously pursuing a strong research agenda and adding scholarly publications and presentations to my portfolio. There were topics that I was interested in pursuing, sure, but I became paralyzed with fear and anxiety when I thought about producing papers for publication. What could I add to the scholarly conversation? Who would want to read anything that I had to say? Past rejections surely tainted my perspective and affected my confidence, even though intellectually I knew that rejection and resubmission were all part of the process. Still, fear got the best of me.

I made small steps in the right direction, but those steps were not adding up quickly enough to get me where I needed to go. I felt myself drifting.

Although I had never aspired to a position as the head of a library or as an administrator, I found that I quite enjoyed that role after I had spent some time learning the ropes from the librarian whom I would eventually replace. However, library administration restructured the organization, which resulted in my appointment to a new position. I was hesitant about the move after having had a few years' experience running a department library with all that it entails, and as a junior faculty member, I did not feel empowered or encouraged to speak up for myself. I think that my biggest challenge was that I knew I needed and wanted help but my pride prevented me from being able to verbalize that need to the right people.

Finding my Balance

With two significant issues challenging me professionally—publishing and finding my place in the organization—I was in need of a clear path forward. As interim head of a department library, I'd become close with a tenured faculty librarian who saw my struggles and decided to rescue me from myself. One day, she pulled me aside and essentially said, "Look, you need help and we both know it. I'm willing to help you, if you are willing to help yourself." There was no denying doing things my way was not working! She shared with me the wisdom of her own experiences as a faculty librarian working toward and achieving tenure. We discussed my career goals, and laid out a solid plan that would help me move forward. So I followed the plan. I worked to develop my research agenda, identified short-, medium-, and long-term project ideas, and decided the best time to work on particular projects. She helped me to brainstorm and revise outlines, proofread drafts as they were written, celebrated with me as they were submitted, and offered constructive feedback on the rejections.

When leaders fail to live up to their responsibility to provide adequate and constructive feedback, opportunities for professional development and career advancement, and so on, these actions may serve as a catalyst for that staff member to change.

Even with dedicated research time built into your workweek, it can be difficult to perform your day-to-day work at a high level and also incorporate research and writing activities, much of which often happens outside a regular nine-to-five business day. It can be a lonely road when family, friends, and non-tenure track colleagues don't understand why "all you do is research and write." It can be a frustrating exercise to continue writing and submitting your work, while dodging the rejection letters that are sent your way. My mentor helped me take control of my career. It is very likely that had I not had someone at that exact point in my professional life who took a genuine interest in me and who was actively involved in helping me to right my ship, I would have ended up on a much different course.

I decided to leave my tenure-track position shortly before it was time for my fourth-year review, the one in which the Appointment, Promotion and Tenure Committee evaluates your progress up to that point, gives you a good idea about the trajectory of your efforts, and indicates whether you are likely to be granted tenure at the sixth-year review. Leaving my position was a tough decision to make. I felt that doing so meant that I was giving up on something I started, like I was letting myself down—failing. On the other hand, it was nothing short of liberating once I realized—with my mentor's insight—that I didn't have to keep traveling that road if my heart really wasn't in it. She reminded me that there is a huge difference between "can't" and "don't want to!" It is deeply empowering to know that you can do whatever it is that you want to do and make deliberate choices that will carry you along the path you choose. I believe that leaders don't allow themselves to simply be carried along with the current. Rather, they take control of their situation and strategically steer themselves to get where they want to go. This was a huge leadership lesson for me. Moving into a position at an institution where librarians do not have faculty status meant being free to pursue my research agenda, but at my own pace, without the "tick-tock" of the tenure clock constantly ringing in my head. It also meant that finding the time to research and write became more challenging as I assumed new responsibilities.

I haven't quite found the *perfect* balance between performing my day-to-day work at a high level, fitting in the time-intensive research projects and taking on various leadership roles in my library and on campus. But I feel that I have found a stable footing so that I can continue making forward progress without capsizing. What initially felt like failure was the catalyst that allowed me to blossom and grow, to plot my course, and to prepare myself to accept new challenges and opportunities. Even now, as a mid-career professional, I still have mentors on whom I can rely when my course gets a bit choppy. I some-

It is very likely that had I not had someone at that exact point in my professional life who took a genuine interest in me and who was actively involved in helping me to right my ship, I would have ended up on a much different course.

times still struggle with my pride, which prevents me from asking for what I need or want, but I'm learning that leaders are rarely alone. They learn from—and grow with—each other.

There is the other side of the mentoring coin, however. As a new librarian, it was incredibly important that I had mentors help guide me early on and now I feel that it is equally, if not more, important to me to serve as a mentor to other young or aspiring librarians. Many times these relationships develop organically and informally; other times they are more structured. I admit to being hesitant to step into the role of mentor, especially since I don't feel that I have it all figured out. This is where mid-career professionals in any area, however, can emerge and shine as leaders.

A few years ago, I had the opportunity to serve as a practicum coordinator for a student who was graduating with her MLIS and needed to complete the culminating experience part of her program. Students choose to write a research paper, carry out an intensive research project, or complete a 150-hour practicum to gain professional experience in a library, information center, or media center. At the time, I was the reference librarian with the least amount of experience at our institution, but I stepped up to serve as the student's primary practicum coordinator. This really took me out of my comfort zone. Though I had some experience supervising staff in my previous position, this was a chance to intentionally serve as a mentor as others had done for me. I wanted to teach and practice the lessons I'd learned along my journey and to help someone else learn to navigate the waters and become part of my professional legacy.

Most of the work that this student librarian did during her practicum was project based. She was able to get a feel for what it was like to work in an academic library reference department while helping us complete projects that would enhance our daily work—primarily the creation of several online research guides. However, as a self-appointed mentor, I tried to stretch my role beyond that of a supervisor. We discussed her future career plans and the appropriate steps she could take to reach her goals; the importance of building a service portfolio at the local, state, and national levels; and strategies to make her education and work experience, including her practicum work at my institution, work in her favor as she competed in the job market with a cohort of other freshly minted librarians. I believe that my influence, however limited it might have been in the short time we worked together, helped her feel supported and that her contributions to our institution and to librarianship as a whole were valuable. Based on what my colleagues and I now hear, I am confident that she is on the path to a successful library career.

Be Scared, But Do It Anyway

In 2013, I was asked to stand for election as vice president/president-elect of the Academic Library Association of Ohio (ALAO). At that time I'd only been a member for about three years, and most of that time was serving as a member of the program committee that helps plan the annual conferences. It was an honor to serve on this committee. It was a great chance to meet and work with colleagues from various academic libraries around the state, and we worked on nearly every aspect of the conference, from choosing preconference and keynote speakers to recruiting vendors, reviewing and selecting session proposals, and setting the final conference schedule. This is no small task for a mid-sized conference that attracts approximately 300 people. It was both fun and stressful, as planning large-scale events tends to be, even if much of my participation was in a supporting role. I also served as a member of a small interest group, where I also helped with program planning; still, that work was also behind-the-scenes.

When I got a phone call asking whether I'd be willing to stand for election for a three-year presidential term, my initial reaction was, "Really? Someone thinks I am ready to serve as president of a whole, entire statewide professional association that I've only been a member of for a relatively short time? Really?!" I was flattered but, honestly, I never imagined that I'd actually win the election. Surely I'd be running against someone with more experience and influence. Surely no one would trust a "newbie" like me with such an important and visible job as the president of a statewide professional association. Surely. I thought seriously about declining the invitation. That way, I could learn more about the association and its work before taking on a three-year presidential cycle.

I spent a lot of time thinking about the "what ifs." What if I said yes? That would be a significant time commitment, starting in the vice presidential year, when I'd be chairing the committee that plans the annual conference— the same committee that I had served on previously. What if I got elected and the conference didn't live up to members' expectations? What if I didn't get elected this time? Would I have a chance to be nominated again? What if I said no? Would that be seen as leadership weakness for failing to serve my association when called upon to do so? Even when I found out I would be running unopposed, I still thought that there was a chance a write-in candidate would sweep the election. Despite having my doubts, insecurities, and concerns, I chose to step outside my comfort zone. I said "Yes."

I saw this as a unique opportunity to expand and solidify my service portfolio at the statewide level. But also, this validated all the career decisions I'd made that led me to this point. I had been so stymied by the research and publication aspect of my previous positions that taking on such a prominent leadership role would have been imprudent and could have really derailed my career. I'd overcome some fairly rough waters since then and was now in a place where I could maintain momentum in my day-to-day work and look farther out toward the horizon.

What became clear to me during the election and my vice presidential year is that we are lucky to be a part of a profession that is full of kind, supportive, very smart people who want to help others. As librarians we are in the business of helping people. I also found out that in many cases, all I had to do is ask for help and invariably people answered, "Yes, how can I help, what can I do?" In ALAO, I am proud to be surrounded by friends and colleagues who want to help me succeed and want to see the association thrive. I am lucky to be in a leadership position where I have many colleagues and partners supporting each other. We're all working for the same goal, and together, we'll get there. Teamwork really does make the dream work.

A Call to Action

While serving as the president of ALAO, I realized there was more I could do for the organization to add to my own leadership portfolio, which included taking a more active role in the recruitment and retention of racially and ethnically diverse professionals in librarianship. Happily, there are excellent programs that can help us address this need. Nationally, the American Library Association's Spectrum Scholarship Program recruits and assists American Indian/Alaska Native, Asian, Black/African American, Hispanic/Latino and Native Hawaiian/Other Pacific Islander students in obtaining a graduate degree and leadership positions within the library profession. There are state-level programs, too, such as ALAO's Diversity Committee, which offers an annual scholarship to a promising student enrolled in an ALA-accredited MLS program who exemplifies the qualities needed to ensure a diverse library workforce. Individual MLIS degree–granting institutions may also have methods of recruiting under-represented students to our profession.

I think we all have a role to play in the effort. Diversity, mentoring, and education go hand in hand. If we work hard to diversify our ranks but don't provide appropriate mentoring and education for our employees, we do ourselves a disservice. For example, if an employee feels alienated, disrespected, and unappreciated in the workplace, he or she may well leave. The organization loses a potentially fantastic employee, as well as some of the diversity that it has worked to recruit. Without the right people in that organization receiving the appropriate sensitivity training, they may fail to recognize the role that they had in his or her leaving. So they hire another racially or ethnically diverse librarian to get those diversity numbers up, but the cycle continues. Unfortunately, part of the problem is that the people who need such sensitivity education the most are almost always the same people who don't think or know that they need it, and therefore aren't in the room when these educational opportunities are offered. This is a perfect chance for library leaders to create safe workplaces in which to retain and develop librarians from under-represented groups, and to encourage librarianship as a career to those who may not have even considered it.

One of my research interests, for which I am currently developing a project, is studying the professional association membership and participation of academic librarians of color, using academic librarians of color in Ohio as a sample group (with the possibility of expanding to a broader geographic area at a later time). Anecdotally, from where I stand as the recent president and current past president of ALAO, it appears that there are relatively few academic librarians of color who are active, visible participants in the organization. If they are members, it's not immediately apparent because I don't see many librarians of color at our annual conferences. Granted, there could be several valid and interesting reasons for this, and I am excited to talk to my colleagues to find out the reasons that they do (or do not) belong to or participate in statewide professional associations, what they value most about membership, and what associations can do to encourage sustained participation, particularly among librarians of color.

That said, I am looking forward to stepping up to a more active and visible level of participation in our national associations, the American Library Association (ALA) and the Association for College and Research Libraries (ACRL). I am excited about becoming a mentor and role model in new ways, helping to promote diversity education in our profession, and widening the available routes to leadership.

Building a Professional Legacy

The thing about a legacy is that we may never know the ripple effect of our actions until the good that we put out into the world comes back to us. I firmly believe that leadership happens at every level, every single day. Whether we are in the classroom teaching essential information literacy skills, participating on important committees on our campuses, serving in elected/appointed positions in our professional organizations, or simply talking with a student who expresses interest and curiosity about pursuing librarianship as a career, leadership can be a part of every aspect of our lives—professional and personal. Our careers may hit rough waters, and we may need to call out for help. We may be called upon to lead, which can be scary. We will most certainly be faced with making crucial decisions at various points where our paths can branch off in several different directions. These crucible moments will invariably shape our leadership outlook and the trajectory of our careers. But they will serve as indicators of just how great we can be if we recognize the opportunities before us and step out of our comfort zones and up to the challenge.

REFLECTIONS: KEY LESSONS FOR LEADERS

» Remain open and ready to accept new opportunities that are presented to you

» Remember that even small-scale leadership can have a big impact

» Recognize that you will need help along the way—use your voice and ask for it

— 15 —

INFLUENCE IS A CHOICE: ALIGNING ACTIONS TOWARD YOUR PREFERRED FUTURE

Peter Bromberg

TOP TAKEAWAYS IN THIS CHAPTER

» Leadership is about our ability to influence. It's about the choices we make in any given situation

» The choices we make and actions we take determine the effectiveness of our influence

» Anyone can exert influence regardless of title or position

Many of us, myself included, do not think of ourselves as "leaders." However, regardless of our title or positional authority, any of us at any given moment or in any situation can get clear insight about what we want and take actions designed to move things in a positive direction. In this chapter I will share a personal leadership crucible that involved challenging a decision by a top state official to end QandANJ, a well-used, statewide virtual reference service. I will review the choices I made and the lessons I learned in trying to generate community support to bring about a positive resolution to this heated issue that played out in public and in the press.

Before we get to that story, however, I'd like to share a key formative experience that helped me develop increased self-awareness and a greater capacity for strategic thinking and resourcefulness, both of which were bedrocks in my ability to navigate the difficult landscape of a public political fight with someone with a high level of positional authority and political power.

Creative, Resourceful, and Whole: Learning to Coach, Learning to Think Strategically

In late 2007 I applied for and was accepted into an Institute of Museum and Library Services (IMLS)–funded program to be trained as an executive coach. The training included one full day and three half days of training, as well as four coaching sessions with a professional coach, followed by meta-analysis of the coaching sessions. A requirement of the program was to agree to offer pro bono coaching to 10 librarians, so there was an opportunity to immediately apply the skills and techniques being learned. The training itself was largely focused on how to use questions and invite reframing to help people think strategically, identify resources, and commit to taking progressive action that would move them in the direction of their goals. Coaching, as opposed to therapy or mentoring, begins with the assumption that the client is creative, resourceful, and whole. The coach's role is to help the client increase their resourcefulness through an intentional analysis of internal resources (strengths, skills, knowledge, etc.) and external resources (allies, funding, reputation, etc.).

The training and practice of coaching provided me with an incredible foundation for understanding how to think through any challenge with an asset-based focus. I learned how to use reflection, writing, and dialogue to help others (and myself) get clear about desired outcomes, take stock of resources, identify potential action steps, and then move into action. The coaching model, in addition to being a solid model of strategic thought and action, was also very much a learning model. After each action, the coach invited the client to assess the effectiveness of the action by asking, "What happened?" and then invited the client to reflect on and analyze the effectiveness of any actions taken. The client then reevaluated their preferred outcome (which may have shifted in light of what they learned from their recent experience), reassess resources, generate new potential action steps, and take new action designed to support their desired outcome.

The training and practice of coaching provided me with an incredible foundation for understanding how to think through any challenge with an asset-based focus.

In my practice with others, as well as in applying this model to my own life, I found that it had fostered a sense of agency and resourcefulness and could lead to very rapid positive changes. Another important element to the coaching model was one of self-care. The first phase of coaching involved identifying elements in one's life that were causing energy drains and then systematically eliminating or mitigating them, while also identifying actions and experiences that are energizing and committing to doing a few of them each week. This practice of intentional energy management reflects the deeper truth that change, even positive change, takes a great deal of energy and that doing intentional self-care is a key part of any change initiative, whether on an individual or organizational level.

Saving QandANJ: Strategies, Actions, and Lessons Learned

The single most daunting and difficult challenge I have faced in my professional career was a struggle to save QandANJ, which was the country's first statewide 24/7 virtual reference service. It was a choice that could put my reputation at risk and potentially damage my career by publicly confronting a powerful state official. This decision required me to think deeply about my core values and decide what I was willing to risk, and why.

In 2000 through 2001 I worked with a colleague at the South Jersey Regional Library Cooperative (SJRLC)—one of four multitype cooperatives in New Jersey at that time—and the staff of 10 libraries to build and launch QandANJ. We began the service with 10 libraries in September 2001, and by 2011, we had expanded to more than 300 staff working at 51 libraries providing over 50,000 online chat reference sessions a year. The customer comments we received were outstanding. Our marketing promotion won multiple awards. Our press coverage was phenomenal, and we had successfully helped libraries demonstrate their value and counter the question of "Why do we need libraries when we have the Internet?" that was increasingly being raised by customers, funders, and the media.

The project was made possible through Library Services and Technology Act (LSTA) funding from the state library, but more so through the thousands of hours each year that each participating library donated to staff the service. The state library, in supporting the project by writing a check once a year, was a valued partner on the funding side and they enjoyed sharing the spotlight and the credit as the service got statewide and national recognition, even figuring prominently in the story when our state librarian was chosen as *Library Journal*'s Librarian of the Year in 2008. Many of the other accomplishments that *Library Journal* highlighted in the "Librarian of the Year" article were projects that were developed and managed by the state's four regional library cooperatives, with the support of state library funding.

By 2010, however, the relationship between the state librarian and the leadership at the regional library cooperatives had soured. There was long-standing tension between the cooperatives and the state library, with state library staff often feeling that they did not receive enough credit for their role and staff at the cooperatives feeling hampered by the state library's more bureaucratic approach and tendency to focus more on political optics than actual impact. This tension came to a head in March 2010 when the state librarian decided to withhold mandated library network funds from the cooperatives, effectively putting all but one of them out of business. I saw this as an attempt to consolidate money and power in the state library, as the state library wound up pocketing the money that had been formerly disbursed to the cooperatives. This also put the state library in a position where they had significantly more power over the ostensibly independent remaining cooperative. After 25 years of great success and valued service to the libraries of New Jersey, the other three cooperatives were effectively out of business by the summer of 2010.

When SJRLC went out of business in the summer of 2010, we took great care to transition the management of QandANJ to Infolink, the remaining cooperative. At that time, funding was in place for the service through July 2011. Through the rest of 2010 and into the first few months of 2011, the state library gave assurances to Infolink leadership that QandANJ would continue to be funded. But in early April 2011, with less than three months of funding left, the state library announced that the service would end on June 30, 2011.

I learned of the decision to kill the service when I received a phone call from a colleague asking if I had seen the announcement. I hadn't seen it, so I quickly jumped on a computer and brought up an e-mail with the announcement. The state library was not simply announcing that it was ceasing funding; it was announcing that QandANJ would be ending. My first thought was, "But it isn't their service to end!!"

I immediately called the executive director at Infolink—the organization that now officially and legally managed QandANJ—to explore ways that we might have a discussion with the 51 participating libraries to determine if they wanted to continue the service and, if so, how we might fund it in the short and long terms. The executive director, however, was not interested in exploring any options for keeping the service going. "The state librarian says the service is ending, so it's ending," she said. I was livid and a bit dumbfounded. Clearly the state library's role during the 10 years of this project was to write a check. But the success of the project was built on the sweat equity and commitment of the 51 libraries and the more than 300 librarians who volunteered their time to staff the service. At this moment, it became clear to me how much I valued an inclusive and participatory approach to leadership and decision making, as opposed to the unilateral approach that was being used by the state librarian. This realization steeled my resolve to not drop the issue but to invest my time and energy to finding a positive, constructive way forward that included the participation of stakeholders in the library community.

As a next step, I reached out directly to the state librarian to suggest that we convene a meeting of QandANJ participating libraries and other interested parties to discuss alternate funding models for the service. In no uncertain terms, she expressed that the service was ending on June 30, period. I attempted to reason with her, agreeing that the decision to withdraw LSTA funding was hers, but the decision to permanently end the service was one in which the participating libraries should have a voice. I also suggested that if the two of us jointly announced a meeting it could heal some of the anger that still reverberated from her decision to defund the regional library cooperatives in 2010. These suggestions were, to put it politely, unwelcome.

It was at this moment, faced with the message that there would be no opening for discussion or

> **It became clear to me how much I valued an inclusive and participatory approach to leadership and decision making, as opposed to the unilateral approach that was being used by the state librarian.**

negotiation, that I realized that any way forward would involve great effort, commitment, and significant investment of time and energy. I knew that tens of thousands of people still used QandANJ every year and I had read thousands of comments from students, single parents, businesspeople, and other patrons who had expressed how valuable it was to them to have a reference service available to them at night. Making a real difference in the lives of real people is what attracted me to librarianship, and working with my colleagues to design and deliver impactful services is what sustained and nourished me as a professional. For these reasons, I knew that I had to push on.

I felt strongly that to pull funding from this successful and heavily used public service with such short notice was highly unprofessional and deeply uncaring of the tens of thousands of customers who used the service. Still, I recognized that it was the right of the state library to choose not to fund it. It was not the state librarian's right, however, to decide whether the service continued. And yet, for the next six months she invested much time and energy in trying to assure just such an outcome.

Assessing, Strategizing, and Getting Into Action

In evaluating the situation, I assessed that there was no political support to be found at Infolink but I believed deeply that the decision to end a successful program like QandANJ should not rest solely with the funder—that the participating libraries and stakeholders in the library community in New Jersey should have a dialogue regarding whether or not this much-used service should continue. Furthermore, if the library community believed that the service should continue, they should be given a fair chance to line up alternate funding. Other states had faced similar situations where state libraries discontinued LSTA funding for services but had given 12 to 18 months' notice to stakeholders to allow them to put together alternate funding models. This was not the case in New Jersey, which violated not only my sense of fairness but my belief that we existed to provide service and value to our customers, many of whom would be adversely affected by this decision.

The IMLS-funded coaching training I had received a few years earlier taught me to strategically identify potential resources and action steps that would be likely to support my desired outcome. Drawing on this training, I thought about where I might find institutional support for a public discussion and identified the New Jersey Library Association (NJLA) Reference Section as a potential resource and ally. I contacted the chair of the Reference Section and requested that the committee convene a public meeting to address whether

In my strategic assessment, the short time line dictated that my best bet for success was to tap into and focus the existing anger in the library community.

QandANJ should be saved, and if so, how we might fund it. Although the chair had received some pressure from leadership in his workplace not to get involved in what could be (and turned out to be) a highly public and occasionally ugly political struggle, he recognized that it was his professional responsibility as chair to call a public meeting of affected and interested parties under the auspices of the Reference Section. The meeting was scheduled for May 13, 2011.

Again, thinking strategically, I realized that there was a very short time line to build awareness of the problem and create pressure on the state librarian to delay or rescind her decision. I made a conscious choice to begin a blogging campaign and use our statewide listserv, available through Infolink, to alert librarians to the issues and the upcoming meeting. It was soon announced by Infolink that they would be discontinuing the statewide listserv. The timing of the discontinuation of the list was suspicious and it was framed as an action taken at the recommendation of Infolink's technology committee. One member of the technology committee assured me that this was not true; however, I suspected that the leadership of the cooperative and or the state library recognized that I was using the listserv to raise awareness and stir the passions of the community around the QandANJ issue. They didn't like the message so they killed the delivery mechanism.

To ensure that I still had an effective way to communicate one-to-many, on the eve of the discontinuation of the statewide listserv I created my own Google group and sent subscription information out as one of the final messages on the Infolink-sponsored list, effectively moving many librarians to the new platform. In my blog posts, I made a conscious choice to adopt an aggressive, angry, and disbelieving tone. This chosen "voice" was well outside my comfort zone, my personality, and my typical manner of speech and action. But in my strategic assessment, the short time line dictated that my best bet for success was to tap into and focus the existing anger in the library community.

My blog posts quickly started being reblogged and talked about, not only in the New Jersey library community, but in the tightly knit virtual reference community across the country. A number of my colleagues in other states left supportive comments on my blog posts, and then found themselves summoned to their bosses' offices because the New Jersey state librarian had called their supervisors (in two cases, calling other state librarians) to express concern about the comments. I received a few phone calls from my virtual reference colleagues who felt that our state librarian's calls had put their employment in jeopardy and that their free speech was being chilled. One colleague asked me to delete her innocuous comment of support.

This behavior from our top-ranking state library official, in addition to the elimination of our statewide library listserv, was beyond the pale and only served to strengthen my resolve. At the same time, it was truly surprising to me that professionalism and ethics—values that were deeply important to me—went out the window. I wondered if I was naïve and recalled an observation by an American politician about the vicious nature of politics when the stakes are small. Increasingly, I was concerned about what damage could be done to my career by people who seemed unbounded by the normal rules of professional behavior. I was also concerned that in a profession that valued niceness, harmony, and a tendency toward conflict avoidance, I might be hurting my chances for future employment by directly confronting a public official. Indeed, I noticed that many colleagues felt very uncomfortable speaking with me about the issue at hand and did not want to get involved.

My blog posts continued to generate attention, and *Library Journal* took notice and published a story that I saw as one-sided and overly deferential to the state library's talking points. I registered my objection to this story with *Library Journal* and they followed up with a second story, which was much more in-depth and balanced. As the story received more statewide and national attention, the state library cast about to provide a reasonable explanation for the discontinuation of the service—something it had not yet done. In the initial announcement the reason given was that "With local libraries experiencing budget cuts it has become more difficult to allow staff the work time to participate." Except this was known as false to even the casual observer as the libraries that actually staffed the service were continuing to do so and the service had plenty of staffing capacity. In an attempt to justify the defunding, the state librarian seized on a 2008 New Jersey Library Association (NJLA) survey of librarians, which was presented as proof that librarians did not value the service. However, the survey information was misrepresented by members of the state library, and the NJLA executive board, which had preferred to stay out of the fight up to this point, convened a special board meeting on the eve of our statewide conference and issued a strong public rebuke to the state librarian. The statement, titled "The Use of State and Federal Library Funds: The Elimination of QandANJ" read in part:

> The NJ State Librarian has two committees with statutory responsibilities in providing direction for the use of state/or federal funds. These committees are the LSTA Advisory Committee and the Library Network Review Board. In order to provide transparency to the library community, the New Jersey State Library must consult with its proper advisory board when budgetary or programmatic changes are to be made. This will give the library community the opportunity to provide input to these critical decisions.
>
> NJLA believes that the decision to eliminate QandANJ should have been presented to the proper advisory board for discussion and input by the library community. The loss of this service has serious implications for the residents of New Jersey and a thoughtful deliberative discussion by the library community would have been beneficial to the library community and the state library.
>
> The New Jersey Library Association expects the NJ State Library to hold an open meeting with the entire library community as soon as possible to discuss the allocation of all state and federal funding. Transparency in the use of library funding is critical for all.

On May 13, 2011, the NJLA Reference Section convened a meeting at the Princeton Public Library. More than 80 librarians, including the state librarian and her staff, attended the meeting. As a direct result of that meeting and the anger directed toward the state library about the short time line and the unilateral decision making, the state librarian agreed to extend funding through September 30 to provide more time for thoughtful planning, review of the service, and (if necessary) an orderly shutdown of the service.

An NJLA task force was soon convened to explore alternate funding and governance models for QandANJ. However, it was now summer, and with a national conference and vacations on the calendar, it was difficult to bring the task force together and conduct meaningful work. Pressure continued to be placed on the state librarian, who agreed to another extension of funding to carry the service through the end of 2011. In the end, the NJLA task force, while finding value in the service, did not have time to line up new funding and QandANJ shut its virtual doors on December 31, 2011.

Conclusions and Lessons Learned

While I was sad that QandANJ did not ultimately survive and believe that the people of New Jersey lost a highly valued library service, I was gratified that the library community had a chance to weigh in. And beyond that, I believe that I performed a valuable service in pushing back against our state librarian, who had been consolidating power into what was already a position that, from a structural/political standpoint, lacked accountability. My efforts to hold the state librarian accountable for her unacceptable actions were personally trying and exhausting, both physically and mentally—not to mention fraught with some danger to my career and livelihood. But I believe that those efforts created awareness among the New Jersey library community and helped foster a healthier political environment that provided checks and balances against future overreach and unilateral decision making.

During the entire ordeal I had the unwavering support of my supervisor, the director of the Princeton Public Library. While many in the New Jersey library community were unwilling to take a position or engage in a public discussion about the state librarian's actions, my supervisor was clear and steadfast in supporting me and the underlying principles of transparency, professionalism, and responsible stewardship of public dollars, which were at the heart of the fight. Her modeling of supportive and principle-based leadership is one of enduring lessons I took away from the experience.

I also learned the value and importance of emotional appeal, and, specifically, the power of anger as a motivational and coalescing force. Accessing my own anger and appealing to the anger in others is about as far outside my comfort zone and natural style as I could get. But—going back to my coaching training—I realized that from a strategic standpoint it was a necessary, if highly uncomfortable, choice. Over the years, I have questioned whether it would have been more effective to focus on a positive vision and try to rally people around an inspirational picture of what could be, as opposed to rallying people against what was. But I've come to believe that the short time line constituted a crisis of sorts and that an appeal to anger was the best strategy to get attention and activate lots of energy quickly— energy and attention that could then be directed to a very specific and easily understood objective.

Another important lesson learned from this experience was the value in intentionally assessing and leveraging my resources. From the beginning of this fight, I was a single person with no positional authority going up against a relatively powerful state official. I assessed my resources as follows:

» **Reputation**: I had 15 years of experience in the library community and was well respected.

» **Social and Emotional Capital**: Related to reputation, I had been generous with my time and had been of service to many in the library community. I had also demonstrated in many professional contexts (association meetings, collaborative projects, etc.) that I was very diplomatic and effective in helping groups and teams resolve conflict and work more effectively together. I had demonstrated a high level of professionalism and had garnered the respect and trust of my peers. There were many "marbles in the jar," as it were, and I could afford to spend or lose some of that amassed capital if needed.

» **Communication Channel**: I had a blog with a respectable following that provided a platform for communicating effectively and efficiently to many people. I also had a statewide listserv (and when that was eliminated, the power to create another one) that allowed me to share links to blog posts through the New Jersey library community quickly.

» **Allies**: I had friends and colleagues throughout New Jersey who were willing to lend their voices, blog spaces, and Twitter feeds in support of my efforts.

» **Official Support:** The support of NJLA, both in convening a public meeting and in issuing a strongly worded rebuke to the state librarian on the eve of our statewide conference, was invaluable in shifting the context of the fight from me versus the state librarian to the the viewpoint that the state librarian was violating core principles of professionalism and librarianship and going against state regulations.

The most important takeaway of this experience was a crystallization of my own understanding of what I was willing to fight for. In my personal and professional life I had no experience in waging this type of public battle. By nature and training I am a peacemaker and a bridge builder. I had never before encountered a conflict where the other party was unwilling to negotiate and was not constrained by the typical boundaries and agreements of professional, ethical, or legal behavior. The situation was unlike any I had ever encountered and thus called for a new and different approach. The entire experience was a crucible that tested my resourcefulness, my emotional strength, and my willingness to place my career in danger. In short, the experience called for a fight, and I learned that I was willing and able to engage in a public, and sometimes ugly, conflict because certain core principles were being violated. The decision to cut a valued service would, first and foremost, hurt the people who relied on that service. Second, I discovered that it was very important to me to stand up against unchecked authority and power when that power was being used in ways that I saw as destructive and unethical.

Ultimately, this experience was an opportunity to take the knowledge and experience I had developed as a coach and apply the coaching model to myself. I practiced self-care and tried to find ways to keep my energy level up during months of an ongoing, public dispute with a powerful person. I learned to think strategically every day and continually assess my resources and the effectiveness of my choices. I learned not to dwell on mistakes and choices that were not fruitful but to learn from them and quickly develop a plan for next action steps based on the reality of the moment. And finally, I learned that "leading from any position" was not just a catchy workshop title; it was an invitation to step up and be fully present in the world and take responsibility for helping create more enriching outcomes through my choices and actions.

REFLECTIONS: KEY LESSONS FOR LEADERS

» Strategic thinking, intentional action, assessment of resources, and continual reflection enhance our ability to exert positive influence

» Exerting influence in difficult situations requires resilience and focus. Intentional self-care is key to maintaining one's energy and emotional intelligence

» Anger can be used positively to generate and focus energy toward a positive outcome

Epilogue

REFLECTIONS ON LEARNING FROM LEADERSHIP STORIES

Steven J. Bell

The cave you fear to enter holds the treasure you seek.

—JOSEPH CAMPBELL

Joseph Campbell may be an unfamiliar name, but his contribution to our understanding of storytelling is the stuff of legend. He is best known for his book *The Hero With a Thousand Faces.* Based on his extensive research into mythology, heroes, and storytelling across cultures, Campbell developed his theory of the hero's journey. There are eight phases of the journey in which the hero undergoes a transformation that results in the realization of a great destiny. These elements of the heroic story are almost always visible in the plot of books or movies that are based on a journey in which the lead character must overcome some difficult challenge to save the day. Many of these stories feature a critical element of the journey, a crucible that confronts the hero. Passage through the crucible ultimately leads to the grand transformation.

Storytelling is among our most powerful methods to share history, to educate, and to inspire. Because stories can also influence our behavior, leaders use them to communicate their experiences and strategies in a way they can benefit aspiring leaders. These same leaders are interested in more than just telling their own stories. They seek out the stories of other leaders, from all walks of life, because they understand the importance of being a leader who is a continuous learner. Not unlike the hero's journey formula, many of the best leadership stories feature a situation in which the leader must enter the cave that he or she most fears.

Like the hero, the leader experiences the trial, a challenging situation that is a test of one's abilities. If the situation requires performance or execution of skills where the leader is mostly untested, he or she will encounter their own fear of failure. This is when the leader may face a crisis, perhaps an organizational collapse, a personnel or building disaster, or unanticipated loss of key resources. If the leader successfully passes through their crucible moment, he or she achieves a resolution of the trial and proceeds to collect the treasure—which may be an opportunity to breathe, relax, and enjoy the moment before the next trial.

Rewards also come in the form of an intangible yet convincing sense of confidence and self-awareness. Whatever glory the leader may bask in in the wake of a victory, the great ones remain humble and reserved, knowing that hubris is the leader's Achilles heel. The hero's journey follows a never-ending cycle of adventure, crisis, and treasures won. Even when leaders encounter a failure, their treasure may be a unique learning experience that better prepares them for that next crucible moment.

Producing a leadership book is a great opportunity to give aspiring and mature leaders new ways to explore and reflect on their own experience and abilities, and come away as a better leader for the time investment. My intent with *Crucible Moments* was to offer a resource that could achieve that outcome in a way that would truly capture the reader's attention, no easy feat in today's world of mass distraction. Asking a group of leaders representing diverse points on the experience spectrum to share their leadership stories seemed the best way to make the most of the opportunity given to enrich the quality of library leadership. I hope that *Crucible Moments* rewarded your time investment with a rich learning experience, one useful for improving the quality of your leadership no matter where you are on that same experience spectrum.

Your experience with *Crucible Moments* is important, but no less essential than the lessons taken away from the contributors' leadership experiences. Despite the diversity of their stories, here are 10 common themes shared across the chapters:

» Few if any early career librarians aspire to lead. When librarians find themselves in a position to lead, those who thrive on the experience choose to continue seeking out opportunities to lead.

» Frontline librarians have mixed emotions about transitioning to administrative positions but believe it affords them the opportunity to implement their unique vision in the pursuit of improving the community members' library experience.

» When the door of opportunity opens, the library leader will walk through it, but leaders make a difference by doing the hard work that positions them to be in the right place.

» Leaders learn from their mentors. Although many leaders participate in a professional development program that matches them with a mentor, mentoring relationships that develop holistically and informally are often the best.

» Leaders give back to the profession by mentoring other leaders. Helping a librarian who wants to explore their leadership potential is among the most rewarding responsibilities that leaders will experience.

» Leaders are risk takers who must deal and be comfortable with ambiguity. If leaders wish to create positive change, they need to set an example for others by demonstrating they are will to take risks in order to achieve gains.

» Leaders promote organizational change not by virtue of the power they have to issue top-down ultimatums but by empowering frontline library workers to participate in the change process.

» Leaders maximize their experience and exposure to learning situations by leading in and out of the library, through participation in institutional or community committees, governance bodies, labor organizations, and professional associations.

» Leaders require time to discover their own voice, which may involve overcoming internal hurdles that may work against us on the path to achieving self-confidence, self-awareness, and a unique vision for library services.

>> Leaders demonstrate an enthusiasm for the future because they believe their work will make a difference in the lives of the constituencies they serve, both internal and external.

Whether I am speaking to a class of students, an audience of librarians or administrators, a gathering of educators, a virtual community of Webinar attendees, or writing a column or article, I am guided by a singular philosophy: Make it about them. That means my intention is completely focused on delivering a great experience to whomever I am addressing via any type of medium. It may be five or 500 people. What matters is making each individual feel as if they were getting my complete attention and knowing that I cared about the quality of their experience. That is the spirit and intent behind *Crucible Moments*.

I hope that I, along with 14 amazing contributors, were able to accomplish what I set out to do with this book—to make it about you and leave you with more than just a great learning experience. If we succeeded, you not only enjoyed reading our stories and the advice shared but you now feel inspired to confront your own crucibles with a renewed vigor and enthusiasm that will enable you to influence colleagues to accomplish great things on behalf of your community. Along the way, every leader will encounter trials and tribulations as well as a few dismal failures. That is the common bond that unites all the contributors in this volume. They all failed at one time or another, but leaders only truly fail when they forget to reflect and take away a lesson that will forge their ability to overcome obstacles, doubt, fear, and the uncertainty that keeps then from realizing their leadership potential.

That is my hope for you: that *Crucible Moments* gets you thinking and inspires you to achieve your full potential as a leader.

Steven J. Bell
Editor

Index